We Are The American Zombies

by

Max Meeks

On Demand Publishing LLC
Seattle, WA 98108

ISBN -13: 9781519437419
ISBN-10: 1519437412

Contents

Introduction

In the 1940's well known behavioral scientist B. F. Skinner was studying how to train animals. He found that through the process of conditioning that their behavior was very easy to control. He quickly realized that the actions of people could be modified as well. The same type of repetition that's been used to manipulate the general public will now be used to empower them. If people are programmable, then it stands to reason that their programming can be re-written.

How many times have you come across situations in your own life where you saw dogs being confined to a pen or even a small cage? These dogs only get a few rare moments of real freedom. The owners of these neglected animals don't think twice about how much time their own pets are actually suffering. Owners will often keep these same loving dogs locked away from infancy until death. That is, unless the dog escapes.

The escaped dog must run far enough away so that the abusive owner can't reclaim their right to keep a loving dog locked down for life. We all know that some dogs have a much worse existence than those that have the run of the house, get a backyard to run in, and get walked daily by a loving owner. Caged and neglected dogs will still greet their owners with wagging tails. Some lives have rare moments of decency.

At the very least, abused dogs cower in fear when their nasty owner shows up instead of charging the owner in an effort to escape. The relationship isn't between equals; there's clearly a master that dominates a subservient dog. All that a dog owner must provide in order to get loyalty is food, water, and shelter. The reason why people love dogs so much is because dogs will accept almost any treatment that we give them with very little pushback. We may have regrets about who we've become, but our dogs help us to avoid these ugly truths. Daily abuses most often go unchallenged.

Abusive and dominating people are always looking for others that they can treat like dogs. How many people do you know that are in bad relationships right now that are there due to guaranteed meals and shelter? Of these people that do put up with tons of unfair treatment for financial security, do you respect them more, or less, for staying?

An army of retirees (holding abundant resources) have been totally terrified by televised terror. Billionaires, the politicians they own, and the very doctors that we've been trained to trust since birth have created an orange pill-bottle army of the walking dead. Just go out to any grocery store and you'll quickly see half-living people riddled with health problems all around you. These defeated people won't hesitate to attack anyone with working brains that actually challenges their TV-trained beliefs.

I dare oppressive and controlling people to try reading this book. Good people will gain freedom and sociopaths will lose power. For decades many Americans were both comfortable, and asleep. That's changing. For those of you that feel stuck in an unpleasant situation, a change in awareness lies ahead.

Chapter 1 – Getting Honest With Ourselves

People with high self-esteems and a healthy amount of self-respect don't stay in abusive relationships. People that like themselves tend to treat others with respect and dignity. It's always those who hate themselves and suffer from low self-esteems that are the most abusive toward others. In many cases the bully has been abused by his or her family members and is totally unaware of why they behave the way that they do. It's sad that most bullies don't even know why they bully. In fact, most bullies don't even perceive that they're bullying at all.

People with low levels of self-control tend to be the worst offenders in their attempts to control and use others. Do you happen to know any people (other than yourself of course) that happen to have very little self-control left? I've met a few, starting with myself.

Admitting that we've lost control in our lives is perhaps the hardest thing for us to do. Our egos lie to us at all costs as we slide down the scale of self-control. The more our addictions take over, the more our egos lie to us about everything. Reality becomes distorted and lies become truth. There's a Grand Canyon-sized gap between most Americans' perception of reality, and the truth.

Over the course of years as a person gradually becomes more and more of an addict, (be it food, TV, drugs, alcohol, or even holy weed) the lies that their ego tells them about their own actions become bigger and more frequent. The obvious addict (to the outside world) that often has a weight problem, substance problem, and uses their addictions to drown out their pain is completely blind to how badly they've lost control. The laws of cause and effect still apply to all of us. Quick easy fixes nearly always deliver long-term impairments.

Somehow the process of addiction truly blinds us no matter how terrible our personal health and quality of living has become. This is only made possible by the function of our egos. A corrupted ego will wreck your body and prevent you from having good relationships with the people that you're most attracted to. This book is deleting those corrupted files so that you can live out your dreams and be happier more often. There will still be ups and downs just as the sun rises and sets, but you'll spend a lot less time feeling like a victim of circumstance.

We're all taught that human beings are given the gift of free will. It's the freedom to make our own choices whether they're good or bad, right or wrong. Free will is our ability to make choices that affect our own destiny. On a different note, dogs have owners.

We all accept that a dog owner decides where the dog sleeps, when and what the dog eats, and pretty much trains the dog to obey his or her commands for the duration of the dog's life. At this point in history there are billions of people that feel stuck in bad situations. Miserable people are really good at enforcing unreasonable working conditions on anyone fearful enough to listen to them. One brave person in a room full of pessimists is a big damn problem. Good slaves for life can get infected with hopefulness and dreams. Ideas create reality and lifelong cashcows can leave abusive owners behind them.

American zombies have been tricked into valuing their dogs more than people. Not so? How many of us look down upon the poor ignorant public as nothing more than millions of selfish, lazy, and stupid people? You know, those nasty Walmart shoppers that are all cheating the system and deserve their awful lives. Many of us have been conditioned to be ok with treating our house pets better than the people around us.

Millions of us spend all of our daily love, compassion, and forgiveness on our pets only. Can you imagine meeting a married couple and having the husband say, "Hi, my name is Bob, and this is my owner Susan?" Sound about right? Where'd that guy's balls go? This is how people act these days and is exactly what our coping mechanisms have done to us. They've turned us into spineless pushovers that nobody respects and everyone abuses (because they can). Nobody truly respects people that lack respect for themselves. Shame shines brightly for all to see.

There are also multiple studies indicating that testosterone levels in American men have been steadily declining since the 1970's. Both our balls and our paychecks have gotten smaller while our politicians have all become multi-millionaires. If a government intended to slowly decline the quality of living across an entire country, (without causing a revolution) do you get that they may have introduced foods and drugs into the population's diet that lower the men's testosterone levels? If I'm a long term government planner that lacks ethics, then I'm going to work smart not hard. Why do you think all of the middle-aged men started needing Viagra? American men have been duped into chemically neutering themselves.

We're all taught and conditioned to drink beer while watching sports on TV. We've been trained to believe that this is the normal thing to do because everyone's doing it. Our TV then shows wall to wall beer and liquor commercials during every sports game. The commercials work and we all know it.

There are millions of Americans that now admit that they're totally dependent upon alcohol. We call them rednecks. They're probably the most honest social group in America when it comes to at least acknowledging their addictions. They're functioning addicts with no intentions of quitting. This is completely opposed to our rich intellectual uncles that stay classy while getting obliterated on wine each and every night.

To the declining economy since 2001 and banks foreclosing on millions of Americans I say, thank you. Billionaires made life painful enough fast enough to actually inspire millions of Americans to try anything. The big banks actually created a fast and hard bottom for millions of good people. Good people with nothing left to lose are now becoming capable of making changes for the better.

Have I personally witnessed other people that transformed themselves in a matter of months by simply removing alcohol from their daily routines? Yes, but there's more than just drinking that's made so many Americans both apathetic and distracted. If you're still paralyzed for three hours a day in front of a TV, (while unconsciously eating) then a fat bloated zombie you'll be. It's now becoming possible to wake up the zombie masses. As a result, filthy rich bankers may finally get to have all of their actions held accountable.

Americans that once would have done anything (while drinking and over-medicating daily) in order to pay for their mortgage, wife, and kids will no longer blindly obey the cruel orders of organized criminals. Why is this now true? In millions of cases the house, the wife, and the kids are gone. Each time this has happened, one more American zombie has been freed from hopeless debt-based servitude. Many of the high-paying jobs now available are so wonderful that they require daily sedation.

Corporations are no longer holding metaphorical guns to our heads. This line of reasoning now applies to millions of decent Americans. We're now refusing to do the dirty work for scumbag bosses at awful jobs because there's nothing left to manipulate us with. We'll no longer abandon our God-given consciences due to this fatal error in bargaining. The 2008 housing price crash could be compared to a lousy magician ripping away a table cloth resulting in all of the plates, glasses, and silverware crashing on the ground. Houses and families once held together during the pre-Obama era are no longer. If you'd like to know how former party supporters became former party supporters, this is it. The financial rug got pulled for millions of people. Their personal trust in government protections is gone.

The still-shrinking upper class seems to be drifting further and further away from reality. In the meantime, the majority of Americans are experiencing more and more pain. The former middle class had been given a huge lesson in humility and something else that the ruling elite know nothing about, a spiritual awakening.

Many of the new lower-class Americans have more daily fulfillment than those that are still clinging onto lifestyle (while hurting others daily to do so). That's the big joke on the drunken and unsatisfied upper class Americans still left. Poorer people are now less enslaved to terrible jobs that are still necessary to cover huge house and car payments. Upper class people have become slaves to their paid-for companionship. If the stuff goes, so goes the families that valued them.

Only people that have already lost everything and made peace with it can understand what a huge joke it is to see miserable rich people possessed by their things. People that worship money (above all else) also frequently suffer from failing health. The frequently bloated ownership class of America is also blind to their now poverty-stricken employees' level of contempt for them. The front line workers of America have lost a ton of respect for the management class still raking in huge profits while acting like they're broke.

America wasn't founded by spineless men and women that accepted every abusive order given to them by their masters. When we start to get honest with ourselves, we can admit that the only reason that people continue on in abusive relationships is because they believe they have no other choice. People that tell others that they're stuck in bad situations are for the most part, full of shit.

In reality, people fail to escape their bad situations due to their own personal fear and lack of any justified confidence. There's no honor in allowing wealthier people to treat you like garbage for money. Self-serving rich people are welcome to keep their giant stash of electronic money and all of the unhappiness and loneliness that goes along with it. The vampire class of America is about to start having a big damn problem, faster food that they can't catch. The public can turn on brand names and products overnight while quality workers leave abusive employers behind them.

We all make daily decisions that create a happy or miserable life experience. We all choose to stay in or leave the situations that we find ourselves in. Assigning all blame to another party while chalking it all up to bad luck is a losing life strategy (that only losers believe in). Every day we're faced with scores of small decisions that fall on the side of self-serving or considerate to others. We're either operating in a conscientious manner, or not. Many people now belong to religious clubs but the majority of their daily decisions are the opposite of what their idol would do. These people tend to have plenty of financial comfort and very little fulfillment.

Happy people tend to believe that they create their own luck. Whether it's positive or negative, we're all creating our own luck as we go. We all know this deep down inside but many of us often drink, drug, over-eat or medicate (guilt free and doctor-approved sedation) in order to perpetuate these lies. When things are going badly, we lie to ourselves a lot.

If there is a God, it's doubtful that this God would prefer that we all cower down before corrupt men and women that happen to have more money than us (in a totally crooked system ran by actual scam artists). Doctors that prescribe anti-anxiety and pain pills to everyone, and then drive home to a huge house in their brand new Mercedes are just about as prevalent and ethical as our politicians. Both groups will do anything to keep driving that Mercedes to their dinner date with their affair.

We all understand that people that have acquired lots of wealth will do all sorts of absurd things to keep the lifestyle. Their egos perform incredible mental gymnastics to justify why they stay rich, and their employees slowly lose teeth. If higher beings do exist, then they won't be impressed with most of us. After all, we're allowing scammers and assholes to rule over us. We're supposed to stand up for ourselves.

When we were all little kids none of us said, "When I grow up, I wanna be a spineless corporate pushover that goes home to a loveless marriage that I'm financially trapped in." Yet, how many people do you know that are only staying with lousy partners due to financial shelter? Do any of those people realize that they're stuck there due to their own perpetual self-sedation?

Pills too transform dignified men and women into heavily restricted vessels. Do any of these people realize that their doctors have gotten them into an active drug habit? More likely these same grown adults that made it into their mid-twenties with no diagnosed mental illnesses now tell the world that they must have their meds.

We're like a bunch of people that purposely pour sugar into our gas tanks because we're about to drive on a retarded highway where the speed limit is 25 miles per hour. Driving around in a sober state of mind with a perfectly running vehicle is simply too frustrating. Slow yourself down and fit-in with the zombies. That's the strategy that most Americans are now going with.

It's not an act of bravery to stay in situations that require daily sedation just to tolerate. How many rich people have you met that seem to be completely miserable and also drink daily? The drunkenness kills their conscience so that they can screw people over all day (to keep that sweet dirty money without feeling guilty about it). Their money and their addictions now drive their behavior. Our society is now being run by mentally ill people that would sooner let the whole country starve than do the right thing. We can't look to corrupted leaders for help. We must save ourselves.

On TV the cops always bust the drug dealers, and the doctors are always making people healthier. When it really comes down to it, for doctors it's all about keeping the house, the car, and the benefits of being wealthy. Screw you, your elderly parents and all of the fat, pale, and bloated zombies that are the actual results of their efforts while earning $100,000+ annually.

If American rich kids aren't willing to destroy the public's health for huge profits don't worry, nightmare third-world countries like India have an endless line of future doctors that have already been welcomed into our system (that's currently run by drug companies). In a global economy, if you can't find local sell-outs to wreck people's health for profit, no problem; scholarships, plane tickets, housing, and a chance to escape poorer living conditions are more than enough to obtain blind obedience. Doctors destroy health, lawyers protect criminals, and priests make sure that the citizens stay obedient to the criminals that now run our government. The first 15 pages of "1984" explained a lot.

Second and third generation doctors have sold us all out to large corporations just as badly as our politicians have. We might as well all be cattle as far as the corporations and billionaires are concerned. They don't see us as equals. After all, they have a lot more money, and as far as they see it, money is God.

Clearly they value their possessions and power more than the people that they're supposed to be serving. Many of the wealthiest people are also some of the most miserable souls. These people are owned, and it's not by God. Television fails to convey that message. Instead, poor people continue clawing at each other in vain attempts to escape their $10 per-hour nightmares.

For years, many of us had higher paying jobs and lived comfortably. Life was good. Money for eating out and entertainment was left over after all of our bills were paid. During the Obama Era, we've been forced to work alongside (and became) paycheck-to-paycheck Americans. Working with down-and-out Americans is like swimming alongside rats on a sinking ship. Low paid workers are extremely guilty of policing each other on behalf of greedy bosses. When disposable incomes disappear, backbiting and every form of treachery become normal. In down economies, decency goes out the window.

Aren't the majority of politicians and corporate CEOs born into wealthy families? What about the rest of us? When on earth are we going to wake up to the fact that the majority of people can't afford to be part of the political process anymore? This includes the upper middle class that's currently under heavy financial attack. By all means this book isn't anti-millionaire. They too are peasants as far as the 1% is concerned. If the political process won't let us participate in a meaningful way, let's deem it invalid and weed-out the corrupt. As long as the majority of the population approves the changes, it's a done deal. Group consensus creates reality. Zombie hordes get what they want.

Millionaires must realize that poor people that are fighting to avoid food stamps are on the same side. Many people still showing up to the only jobs still available are now poor. If this country falls apart and turns into a giant welfare state, then it's going to be a nightmare for all of us. Perhaps all of us do have the right to limit how much wealth (power) one person is allowed to have. We don't want billionaires limiting the size of sodas or telling us what we can or cannot eat for lunch. That definitely is happening in the U.S. right now and violates our freewill.

We keep allowing billions of human beings to suffer, so that one person can point to a number on a computer screen and tell his friends, "I've got more than you." If we're being honest, bragging rights and world domination are pretty much the only reasons to start competing against other billionaires. Zombie Americans are now serving the few and their own minority agendas based on greed. Nationwide wages prove this.

If we were all monkeys in the jungle, it's as if a few monkeys have picked all the trees bare (leaving no bananas for the rest of us). The result being, a few gluttonous monkeys now control a giant stockpile of rotting bananas that's being guarded by idiots with machine guns. This is exactly what billionaires on planet earth are doing to the rest of us right now. Their spoiled-rotten children then get honorary jobs where almost zero work is done while receiving a tax-funded paycheck. This is what's happening. Rest assured, these token-holding workers have active drug habits making them believe their own bullshit. The rest of the taxpayers then pick up all of the slack while losing health benefits along with their teeth. It's clear that 3rd world conditions are now present in our labor force when 30-50 year-olds are losing teeth. These American workers aren't healthy, they're dying.

We all must realize that there are billions of us and only thousands of them. Until billions of us figure out how to regain control against a few thousand men, then we might as well be living on the planet of the apes. If I'm forced to choose a team, then I'm choosing team ape. We aren't that smart as a group, but after some small individual changes we can begin working together. When doing so, even tyrants can be removed with ease. There are appropriate times in history for the masses to revolt against an increasingly brutal ruling class.

Only addicts and cowards keep taking degrading treatment from selfish people without standing up for themselves. If you aren't a coward, yet you still find that an honest look at your own personal situation reveals that things have become a lot worse; then

14

perhaps it's about time to sober up and start making things better in your life. A lot of good people stay in horrible situations only for as long as they're on chemical crutches. It's about time that we drop the crutches, have our come-to-Jesus moment, and start walking across the stage.

There are some bad people in this world. It's time that we bring their bad deeds out into the light. Countries full of oppressed citizens only exist due to a majority of cowardly people. The quality of living in America was only made possible by brave people that organized and rebelled against tyrannical leaders. Taxation without representation prompted civil disobedience. As always, civil disobedience then draws military occupation. Isis attacks are just the excuse to put the troops in place. A disobedient tax base already exists.

Chapter 2 – The Root Of The Problem

People with low self-esteems don't like themselves (whether it's for good reason or not). A healthy person with a good attitude can be mistreated enough times by enough people around them to eventually believe that they're worth less. Smart and talented people can get treated like gold in one city and trash in another. The daily feedback from the people around us has a huge effect on how we feel about ourselves. Where do we see and hear nearly every piece of bad news that will affect our country's diminishing quality of living?

TV is the one common thread that unites (divides) the American people and informs (dictates) our ever-worsening circumstances via a continuous drip-feed of controlled information. We're all told so in a very matter of fact manner every day of the week by a screen in our homes that strongly influences our buying behaviors. Do you really think that millions upon millions of people would be buying there 2nd, 3rd, and 4th I-phones for hundreds of dollars if it weren't for the power of advertising?

Any halfway sane person that isn't 100% blinded by ego will admit that TV ads do work. I want to buy some European hair remover called the "No No" after just 3 or 4 repetitions of their commercial. Whoever can afford the most TV time can then sell us whatever they want to. Shoot the con-man dead by turning off your TV.

We don't like being sold something that we didn't need before the salesman con-vinced us to do so. Somehow the world's slickest con-man ever to get past our front door and into our living room, family room, bedrooms, and bathrooms has successfully done so in billions of households worldwide. We all keep buying ideas that have failed to make our lives better. In fact, most peoples' lives are now getting worse in direct proportion to hours spent in front of their TVs.

We keep on buying lies from our politicians and somehow we keep the thing on that's been selling them to us. Do you ever remember being convinced of WMDs? Did they ever exist in our minds before the TV told us that they were there in Iraq? **We Must be Dumb.**

We buy into all kinds of new products and ideas that our TV has trained us to believe would improve or threaten our lives. Our TVs have conned us into trying tons of new products and services. Did anyone else out there get that exercise bike or that indoor snow skiing machine? We've all been tricked at one time or another by a too-good to-be-true product. Most of us never did get the six pack abs promised to us by the miracle sit-up machine.

The pills that promised us long walks on the beach with good looking sexual partners have failed as well. Unless both partners worship in the same church of the holy pill bottle; that good looking date on the beach is long gone when they discover a medicine cabinet full of peace and spirituality. Replace that feeling of spirituality that drinks and pills have given us with something more accurate. Delusionality: a non-threatening state of existence to other delusional people. Cult members feeling comfortable while surrounded by other cult members or drunks in bars surrounded by other drunks are all comforted by similar people. Are both daily drunks and daily cult members at least a little bit delusional?

Nobody wants to deal with the side effects that any drug addict or alcoholic cannot escape. There are no magic pills or drinks. The only thing that those pills deliver is a greater likelihood of weight gain, selfishness, premature aging, and increased apathy to do anything about it. They're a trap that down-and-out citizens across the world are caught in.

Cults that practice daily rituals and convince their members that they've gained the moral high-ground also produce delusional people. Our society has been carefully divided into different cults of Americans that are equally delusional about their own cult's level of morality. When we grow up attending a particular church, it all seems normal. The sheer repetition of just about anything can make an insane ritual seem normal. We see this in other cultures around the world. Tremendously stupid traditions are common and humanity really isn't that bright. I wish we were, but we're not.

Therefore, depending on them to do the right thing and save you (while using your hard-earned tax dollars) is a losing belief. Leaders gain wealth while workers lose teeth.

In a true act of insanity we continue to go out and buy the things that our TV teaches us all about. This has resulted in a country that is now fatter, dumber and poorer than we were just ten years ago. It's as if half of the country has been hypnotized into a barely conscious condition. Most Americans are unable to refrain from the next unnecessary and over-sized meal. It's nearly impossible to avoid scores of half-crippled and totally defeated people hobbling toward their next feeding in pain. The movies simply over-exaggerated the normal zombie symptoms: pale, bloated, not so bright, and constantly hungry. Isn't this what we see every day? Why on earth would a person choose to become like this? Is it really a choice at all? Is it possible that we've been conned into this weakened version of ourselves?

The conman is your TV. The belief that pills and alcohol will deliver peace and better relationships is the con. Unscrew the cable cord and the conman is neutralized. After doing so, we can regain our health and quit buying crap we don't need. We all know a group of people that will say anything to gain our trust and then take our money and not deliver. Where exactly do we see and hear from these people?

Television has conned people into believing that they are powerless over their own sad set of circumstances in life (which isn't true at all) and that the majority of their hardships have been caused by members of the opposite party. A few hundred million Americans have been convinced to believe in this line of logic. We believe that our party has the moral authority and that most problems in America can be blamed on the other cult-like party. Both parties have failed to deliver on their promises for decades.

If you do everything that your idol on TV wants you to, and they break all of their promises after being elected, then why would you keep participating in that particular con? If I have regular attendance at a church and pay my weekly offerings, (taxes over the course of years) and that church fails to deliver on any of its promises, (while taking my time, attendance, and money) then I quit going. If enough other church members also decide to leave because all of the healthy church members have vanished, then the church goes out of business.

The same preacher that failed to make good on his promises after taking other peoples' money for years might have to struggle financially like his sheep-like followers did while supporting him. Now that's some change that I can believe in. Our politicians deserve no less. The fact that individual Americans donate a penny while corporations are making all of the new laws is a joke. TV watching Americans from both political parties are sheep-like parishioners foolishly looking to their cult-like leaders for salvation. Everyone that hasn't been hypnotized by sociopaths on TV knows that salvation lies within. Small children could decipher such obvious scams but grown adults are failing to.

The more television that a person is exposed to, the more powerless that person feels (because of the beliefs that their TV has sold to them). I began noticing these hopeless zombies walking all over the city of Cleveland, Ohio after relocating from Atlanta, GA. Anytime a person becomes accustomed to one culture and then relocates to a new area, the differences between two cultures become painfully obvious.

I specifically remember coming across a middle-aged fat man inside of a Sears store. I told the plump man how I'd moved back to Cleveland after living in Atlanta. I stated that it felt like I had moved into an entirely different country. I was unapologetic while stating how much happier and more hopeful the Atlanta residents were than the grizzled Clevelanders. The plump man in a very matter of fact manner stated that Cleveland would beat the hope out of me in less than a year. He was wrong.

I believe the term indoctrination is what the plump man was attempting to project onto my future. Luckily, I have found a way to shield myself from these dog-conscious people and convert their apathy toward the fallen middle class into fuel for creating a solution. In the fat man's defense, after twenty years of watching his home teams and local economy get demolished, he had been conditioned to be less hopeful. Many of us have become just like him without even being aware of it. Do you want to be like the fat man, supplying a voice of doubt to those that are younger and more hopeful than yourself?

Anyone that's conditioned to lose over and over again (during the course of years) eventually, hopes less. After a while, supposedly free people start acting a lot more like prison guards and inmates. Nearly all of the young working class of Cleveland (absent of wealthy parents) are assimilated into the lower-class culture. They can easily be identified by their tattoos, drunkenness, drug-addictions, and anger. My persistent and vocal refusals to comply made me a very unpopular guy in the lunch room. As a result, many meals were missed while there.

A vast majority of the lower class 18-55yr olds end up smoking cigarettes and getting covered in tattoos to let the world know what a tough life they've had. Cleveland sure did look like a giant open air prison to me. It pained me to see an entire city of people divided into drunken, tattooed, smoking inmates while the clean-cut, non-tattooed, non-smoking upper-class viewed the rest of the population as trash. It was a whole city consisting of guards and inmates.

We're all valuable, but the Cleveland upper-class didn't see it that way at all. They somehow fancied themselves as some sort of royalty. They truly believed that they were just a little bit smarter and a little more deserving of a pleasant life than the rest of the inmates. The retirees of Cleveland were severely delusional about the rapid decline of their once decent city. Sadly, they too had been blinded by the hypnotic trance that their TVs had put them in. This is no different amongst senior citizens nationwide. In manufacturing cities like Cleveland, many of the middle class college grads have fled.

When a city or entire population acts shamefully, we shouldn't be afraid to speak about it. Some places are hellholes. If that's where you choose to stay, then that's where you deserve to be. Is North Korea a hellhole? Did Communist Russia have millions of people living in extremely impoverished conditions?

Does Detroit, Michigan exist?

We've established that dogs do have owners. What if billionaires devised a new strategy to have slaves but called them by a different name. Something that sounds more respectful. Something to make them feel like they have much more control in their lives than they actually do, and something that gives an illusion of control over their tax dollars. Something like, voters.

These voters will become part of a system that over the course of time becomes entirely controlled and owned by billionaires (from behind the scenes). These voters will be divided into two opposing sides each of which is carefully trained via TV to blame all of their problems on the opposing side (instead of the billionaires that have hijacked the system). The super wealthy will completely determine all political policy that the voters don't (at all) care for, but must remain compliant to.

Most Americans are totally unaware of how badly television has clouded their judgment and programmed their beliefs. Imagine if the American zombies were all persuaded to watch the uninterrupted movie of George Orwell's "1984" followed by wall to wall TV coverage the next day announcing that TVs will now be called Big Brothers. Also, all televisions must be kept on at all hours of the day (for our safety of course) by law and punishable by prison. Everyone must also wear a tracking bracelet (Apple I-watch) at all times just so Big Brother can constantly know your location (and even listen in if you raise any red flags). I mean, it's not like smartphones are already doing exactly that.

I can see the conversations between the stupidest people in America the following days saying, "Aw shit! You've got a 60 inch Big Brother in your family room! Damn! I only got a 40 inch Big Brother in my family room! I'll bet that 60-inch Big Brother trains the shit out of your thoughts! In just a few months, I'll bet your ass will be gettin fat as shit, dumb as shit, and as fearful and hopeless as shit!" Idiocracy.

Nothing would be funnier than giant piles of broken flat screen TVs deposited in our billionaire slave owners' front yards to let them know that all of their dogs have finally realized how to take off their mind-controlling collars. If television is the primary delivery tool for installing fear-based beliefs and establishing a group consensus; this fear-based system of control must prevent voters (the peasant class) from standing up to the lying politicians.

Tyrants and slave owners depend heavily on a general doubt of God and a strong fear of death to manipulate the most voters (suckers) possible. If there were events that proved beyond the shadow of a doubt that human beings have a soul and that there are higher spiritual beings (100%, for sure) then people would lose their fear of tyrants. Why do you think that organized religion is so completely un-appealing to the average person? I love God, but I hate church. Mission accomplished.

Our Politicians have used the TV to instill (install) terror into our imaginations. These terrorists were literally funded and armed by our own elites to destabilize their competition in foreign countries. Then, the same threat that our billionaires funded is used to put more surveillance on the American public. For our hopeless neighbors that always say, "It is what it is" ISIS became the re-branding of CIA funded terrorists (formerly known as al-Qaeda). Look it up.

We all have our own hopes, dreams, and imaginations. Rich sociopaths are using television to tell us the way that things are, and the way that things should be (according to them). It's a total scam run by selfish people that don't care about the public (at all). They want us to stay poor while working 50+ hours per week (at two part-time jobs) while they go golfing daily and see the general public as trash.

Picture a scale that's totally loving, forgiving, virtuous, and brave at one end, and totally selfish, heartless, sociopathic, and fearful on the other. Most of us fall somewhere in the middle just on the side toward goodness (but with plenty of room for improvement). We're supposed to be learning from our past mistakes and trying to work our way closer to the good side of this scale (without going overboard). Don't play Clark Kent for a world full of voters. If you do, they'll quickly unload their unwanted responsibilities onto you. Zombies love doormats and will bite anything that's living.

Television (tell-a-vision) has reinforced the belief that sociopathic behaviors result in greater personal wealth. TV also sells us the illusion that wealthier people are enjoying their lives more than the rest of us are. They're not. Most rich people are miserable and are always chasing after the next thing. They're like dogs chasing cars. There's no meal or win that's large enough to deliver them long-term satisfaction.

Working class people that gain true enlightenment would have no more fear of death and become damaged goods in the eyes of abusive owners. Concrete evidence of life after death would completely undermine fear and guilt-based control systems. There are books about near-death experiences where non-believers are suddenly and miraculously convinced of an afterlife. They exist. Those with true spirituality can't be forced to do horrible things.

People with true faith and failing health wouldn't be throwing hundreds of dollars a month at prescription pills to painfully stay alive if they actually trusted that nothing scary was going to happen after death. These types of fearful people are lying not only to the group but to themselves. We've been mind-controlled to fear death by our organized religions and by the con-men that have infiltrated them.

Rulers want the average man to intensely fear going to hell or or to believe in nothing at all. The whole point is that the public loses faith in God and instead seeks protection from their governing officials (lying politicians) that funded the overseas terrorists in the first place. This all takes place while the public is too high, too medicated, and too hypnotized by television to see how the scam is working. Only our own stubborn pride and the weakened processing power of a TV-addicted and medicated brain that allows the con to continue. The Bushes, Clintons, and Obamas gain more control over our lives, and we continue to grovel to them for more protections.

If an entire army of voters suddenly lost their fear of death, then the slave owners would have no one left to do their dirty work. Keep shoveling crap everyone. Organized religions have been filtered and controlled by governments for thousands of years. Entire books have been removed from the Christian Bible (such as: The Book of Enoch). The scientific recovery of the Dead Sea Scrolls proved this beyond the shadow of a doubt. Any smart king would be sure to remove ancient books that undermine his own authority. Have you ever heard of the King James Bible?

Even the History Channel has been leaking these little-known facts into the awareness of the American public. Can you think of any organized religions that make their followers feel guilty? Nearly all organized religions have impossible to follow rules when combined with our current political and financial systems. The logical computers in our brains are totally crashed by these contradicting belief systems. Our church, the TV, and the declining economy that we have to survive in all completely contradict one another. As a result, we're living in a world where honest people are subservient to assholes. That seems to be the opposite of what God would want.

Two or more contradicting orders being given at the same time by different authorities make a brain crash. When two bosses (that can both fire us on the spot) give us conflicting orders at the same time in front of each other, we freeze. This is what the combination of organized religion, television and our current job market has done to the brains of the American public. Our hard drives have crashed and this book is unfreezing them.

The processors in millions of our heads have slowed down badly because we're damned no matter what we do. The only way that most of the working class people can keep functioning in an insane system is to intentionally turn off their logic via alcohol or guilt-free prescription drugs (pill-form alcohol). Does that sound about right? To deal with insane logic, you must turn off the logic in your own head on a daily basis. Booze, weed, and prescription pills do a great job for this.

Aside from religion, kings came up with an ingenious tool for manipulating people to behave against their natural consciences, money. Stop and think about how many times you've seen otherwise reasonable people commit shameful actions in the pursuit of obtaining or protecting their money. For a lot of people, money has become God. After all, our televisions and life experiences have conditioned us to believe it.

If you'd told somebody 100 years ago that wealthy men would build a device that conned the masses out of nearly all of their time and energy (and turned them into mind-controlled slaves) the billionaires would probably ask this question...Why? Why would people allow such a device to stay in their homes? How could this device escape detection from the targeted audience?

Imagine a villain giving a radio-active vase to his next target. The bad guy puts the expensive vase right in his unsuspecting victim's family room. Unless they own a Geiger counter, the vase continues to do damage to the whole family (slowly ruining their health over the course of years). If something is gradual enough, it can evade detection from the smartest of people.

We've all been trained to worry about terrorists from thousands of miles away. In the meantime, we're getting the message from a biological weapon that we've voluntarily paid for. We sit in front of it for hours a day while it slowly robs us of our freewill and plants powerful ideas and beliefs into our minds. Voters (peasants with no real say) will be trained to believe that the TV is strictly for entertainment and information only. People will also be trained (sub-consciously) to attack any person that proposes to them that television is mind control. They'll attack those people that have broken free from the daily hypnotizing without even realizing it.

With enough repetition, even a lie can become the truth. It wasn't that long ago that we all lived on a flat planet. Try not to be one of the ignorant mob that cheers on while your round-planet neighbor gets locked up or hanged for saying so. It's happened throughout history. Crowds of angry fools are used to shout-down and haul-off the first people exposing the latest cons of the current tyranny.

Chapter 3 – The King's Angry Mob

Sky scrapers being demolished into giant clouds of dust on September 11th 2001 by airplanes that were hijacked with box cutters, escaped NORAD's space-age technology missile defense system, and were manually flown into tall thin buildings by crappy amateur Cessna pilots at 500 miles per hour, was and is one of the greatest lies ever sold to the public. To speak out against the official media accepted 911 story and attempt to reason with an average person using facts, logic, and evidence is asking to make many (less now) Americans angry. TV has badly brainwashed the public to attack their own fellow Americans for even attempting to ask questions about 911 that beg to be asked. This is changing.

Not two but three buildings in New York City were obviously rigged up with explosives and demolished on the day of 911. Evidence of thermite (a high temperature explosive) used to cut steel beams was found at ground zero along with video evidence of cut beams. Yet, to point out the in-your-face evidence that contradicts the official (government official) version is to get yelled at by the dazed gameshow-watching zombies. Instead, we're told by government officials that it's anti-American and unpatriotic to humor such conspiracy theories (CIA term). This line of logic was delivered on TV by George W Bush about 911. Do people have a high or low opinion of that man's honesty and intellect?

When we stop getting high or popping mind-melting pills every day, then our perception of the world around us changes completely. Do you think that a completely sober person's perception of reality is more or less accurate than an addicts? After all, what do architects, engineers, pilots, doctors, psychologists, and actual video evidence mirroring every other controlled demolition in recorded history matter if our politicians have explained the whole thing away to us (just as accurately as they explain away every tax dollar)? There's always a BS excuse, they failed to protect us, and they need more money to do so.

I'd rather be spiritually awake with a functioning conscience than too afraid to speak out against the (frequently braindead) public. We know that we've lost respect for each other so why should I worry about this particular group's opinion of me for any longer? This line of reasoning applies to all of our speech. The group isn't that bright, nor even coherent. We're all told to be politically correct at all times to avoid offending full-blown morons and actual drug-addicts. It's as if crazy homeless people are the only Americans left with free speech.

Jet fuel from the planes that hit the twin towers (and not building #7 that collapsed at 5:30pm with no plane impact) burns at around 1700 degrees F. The steel framework of the buildings (woven together and still intact after each plane impact) melts at around 2700 degrees F. Other steel skyscrapers have had raging infernos that burned for hours and hours and didn't collapse into piles of fine dust. Also note that these buildings were filled with asbestos (which would require an ultra-expensive renovation).

Thermite (an explosive) was found at ground zero and burns at around 3000 degrees F. This is enough to cut through the steel beams as the video evidence in the days following the disaster suggests. Also note that days after the Twin Towers collapsed, molten steel was found under the rubble at the bases of the buildings. Many NYC fireman and rescue workers are on video testifying of the molten steel.

The owner of the Twin Towers Larry Silverstein (who had signed a 99 year lease just 6 months earlier for 3.2 Billion dollars) profited greatly from the event. The insurance was only supposed to pay out 3.5 billion dollars, but, in 2007 Mr. Silverstein was awarded a settlement of 4.55 billion dollars. He tried to collect more by claiming each building individually. In all, buildings that had required a massive asbestos removal costing roughly 200 million dollars and had been banned from demolition by the New York City Port Authority (due to their asbestos content) had been successfully (and profitably) removed. When it was all said and done, the building lease holder had turned a 1+ billion dollar profit in just 6 years.

A young film maker made a movie called "Loose Change" that completely contradicts the official (government official) 911 story. Millions of Americans have now seen the documentary. Those whom haven't are behind the learning curve. Had the movie been proven to be slanderous against the super wealthy people that are implicated, then the film maker would have been legally ruined, but wasn't. If the average person even thinks about going to battle against a billionaire, then the average Joe will get legally decimated. Unless that is, their claims and evidence are so damning in the public eye that the billionaire is best to stay quiet and suppress attempts to communicate the truth to the public.

Ask NBA owner and billionaire Mark Cuban if threats from the SEC and powers-that-decree are a joke. Cuban intended to fund a nationwide release of "Loose Change" in theatres, but withdrew from the project after legal ruin and possible incarceration were threatened against him. He then withdrew support for the documentary, legal threats from a publically-agreed-upon corrupt government were dropped, and he remained a (less) free man. Allow the profane to attack and ridicule their intelligent peers for the crime of curiosity, and quietly live on with a new sense of shame for not being allowed to say that 2+2=4.

Those who even humor the possibility that billionaires would lie to the public should try Google searching "911 Truth" and see what you find. Google has most likely buried the results. Just because the mainstream media sets up one Straw Man celebrity (Charlie Sheen) that questioned the validity of 911, doesn't mean that Dick Cheney's version of the story is the truth. Do you remember both Dick Cheney and George W Bush getting to testify together to the 911 commission, in private, together at the same time, not under oath, and off the record? That's what happened. The financial meltdown of middleclass America in the years following made such inquiries a low priority.

Multitudes of brilliant people worldwide completely disagree with the official 911 story. We all agree that the public is full of idiots so why wouldn't government psychologists use proven tactics like the Straw Man argument to squash public curiosity?

Burying our heads in the sand and uncontrollably yelling at strangers attempting to present new information to us (while calling them conspiracy theorists) ought to be disturbing to us. Stop and ask yourself, "Why did I get so angry at them?" Do you realize that television has trained us to become the thought police?

Billions of dollars were made by multiple individuals after the 911 events took place. I see people lie for hundreds of dollars. Plenty of people have murdered and been put in jail over thousands of dollars. Why is it that the public finds it so hard to believe that a handful of evil people wouldn't be capable of sabotage when billions of dollars could be made? War profits, government coups, and oil rights are easily worth billions of dollars. We also know that wicked people seek positions of power.

We've seen our politicians lying to us over and over again for decades. Why wouldn't our politicians be capable of carrying out just one more momentous lie amongst a lifetime's worth? To accept that such a thing could happen in America is very upsetting. However, people living in other countries from around the world don't have such a hard time accepting this.

How was the American public not outraged when our 10% approval rating Congress formed the 911 commission and found that no government officials had messed up? Their report never even mentioned building number 7 (the 3rd New York City skyscraper that was demolished on the afternoon of 911) and has eluded the zombies' awareness entirely. Having our politicians investigate an attack on our country would be like having a bunch of mobsters investigate an attack on a competitor's casino in Vegas. Also, when questioning two different Mob bosses from the same family; the public would be just fine if we allowed them to be cross-examined in private and together in the same room at the same time, while not under oath. It makes no sense, but that's what happened. Wouldn't you know it, no governing officials were found at fault. Weird, they normally take complete responsibility when failing to protect us while living lavishly (funded by us).

How long's it going to take for the American public to accept that our politicians aren't our protectors? They keep piling up their own wealth while the middle class disappears. Even hardcore democrats like Nancy Pelosi are now worth tens of millions of dollars. Look it up. It's all a huge sham and we're funding it. This is obvious to anyone that's not constantly sedated. At the very least, they're the farmers and we're the sheep and cow-people. We're now being milked and sheared more frequently while kept in smaller pens with worsening food, hence grocery store workers' teeth falling out. Banana republic America is here, and now. Go to the most corrupted states and look at the health of their workforce. In many cases, both their health and their teeth are crumbling.

We've been trained to hear the words "conspiracy theorist" attached to any news item at all and then immediately accept the politician-approved version of the story. Both parties seem to always get caught lying to us. Only flawed logic and a delusional ego would allow someone to keep plowing through life without addressing this obvious problem. We've been programmed to accept lies while attacking more credible voices of reason.

There are intelligent people that outperformed their classmates and are excellent problem solvers. However, when these same bright people attempt to shed light on the truth about a phony-sounding news story, we've all been conditioned to call them a conspiracy theorist (thought criminal). These same smart people have a much better track record of truth than the billionaires that now own all of the news networks.

If one thing is for sure, it's that all billionaires must be the most honest and ethical while acquiring 999 times one million dollars in assets. Several hundred million simply isn't enough to feel successful. We're allowed to limit how much power one person has. These are flawed human beings just like the rest of us, not gods. Humanity is fully entitled to remind any billionaire of this. If we so choose, we can strip them of their power in an instant. There are billions of us and not a whole lot of them.

We'd better get things back to where reasonable people are running the show before billionaires build robot armies. It sounds ridiculous I know, but there are already robot planes (drones) that blow their enemies up now. Ask civilians living in Pakistan if this is a joke? Training not-so-bright kids from the ghetto (former nice suburbs) to carry out remotely-controlled murder has already been done. Mission Accomplished. As for robot armies, watch videos of violent protestors attacking innocent elderly bystanders in public and you may realize that robots already exist. Tyrants don't need robots, they already own all TV-programming.

We're only stuck in this worldwide servitude system for as long as we remain a collective group of victims. We could require that all tyrannical billionaires be stripped of their assets due to crimes against humanity. In the light of concrete evidence (which is out there) most people reading this would argue on the side of justice. We do want billionaires with no conscience to be removed from power, right?

We could offer them all jobs at McDonalds, life in prison, or allow them to graciously blow their own brains out. Once again, this is only when their close business partners, friends, and family provides evidence of crimes against humanity. There are plenty of underlings out there that do understand just how dirty their bosses are (Jeffrey Epstein). These people haven't been very nice to the rest of us, and we're failing ourselves by remaining subservient to scumbags.

Tell-a-vision has successfully trained the majority of us to call critical thinkers conspiracy theorists. Does anyone not see the similarity between George Orwell's 1984 and the present world that we now live in? It's become impossible for intelligent people to reason (using logic) with their neighbors about any information that hasn't already been broadcast on television to the entire hoard.

We've become an entire country of battered wives smacking away any hand that tries to pull us out of our abusive relationships. We keep telling people that the politicians love us, but guess what, they don't. The rich kids wearing expensive suits that investigated 911 don't care about you and they never will. They have nothing but contempt for the American public. Why? It's because we're acting like marks that prefer being lied to. Self-respecting people with the guts to confront those that steal from them would never put up with such obvious corruption. Leaders will only act honorably when they fear repercussions from the group. When the group acts like cattle, so will they be treated.

We've been acting like a bunch of cowardly lions that have accepted more and more abuse over the course of decades. We've become more apathetic with each generation. "Hard times create strong men. Strong men create good times. Good times create weak men. And, weak men create hard times." G. Michael Hopf. The only way for any of us to get any real relief is by ending relationships with things, substances, and people that no longer serve us. We must first sober ourselves up in order to regain the guts and brains necessary to create lives worth living. For me, removing TV programming delivered the biggest gains to my baseline of consciousness.

Over the course of time we've allowed and consented to whatever our government is and has become. All of us are partly responsible for what our country has become. For years of my adult life I was guilty of letting somebody else deal with it. Not anymore. I dare to speak out when a rubbish-sounding news story is broadcasted to my group. I've been ridiculed for doing so, but the group is too dangerous when we allow con-men to speak uncontested. Calling out liars and cheats is the honorable way to live. This type of behavior isn't accepted in banana republics, and I don't wish to live in one. Free speech and bravery make life difficult for dictators.

Anyone that hears the words conspiracy theorist (that condemnation toward any actual intellectual curiosity) regarding subjects not government-approved and drip-fed to the zombies via television gets a negative emotional reaction. Why do we ridicule these theorists for thinking? Why is questioning the honesty of our politicians' televised version of the truth a bad thing? Is it possible that we've become an entire nation suffering from Stockholm Syndrome?

Do battered wives get angry and start defending their abusive husbands when friends and family try to reason with them to leave? Only after a severe beating will a battered wife even consider leaving. Do we really like rich men in suits on TV dictating a rapidly declining quality of living to an army of three hundred million zonked-out Americans? Just like the people in "1984" we've been trained to attack those seeking truth and asking questions.

We yell at our friend, neighbor or co-worker that's always been good to us if they so much as mention a non-government-approved thought. We then defend the official congressionally-approved version of the story that billionaires and politicians have investigated themselves. We're a country of marks (soon to be Marxists). It never ends well.

Maybe we should try unplugging our cable box for a month and see what happens to our belief systems. Let's see what happens to our level of anxiety and how often we're thinking about terrorists. The processors between most American ears have been infected with a virus that somehow keeps us trusting a bunch of con-men in suits. See if you side with a millionaire in an expensive suit, or your next door neighbor that's never been caught lying to you after you've unplugged your TV for an entire month. The battered wife analogy will make much better sense if you do so.

We've been lied to by rich men's PR agents for decades. We call them politicians and newscasters (script readers). Every time that we throw one crook out he's immediately replaced by another agent in a suit coming from a seemingly endless line of con-men. How the public could miss the point of an endless supply of the agent Smith character in "The Matrix" movies is beyond me. Once you're in a dictatorship, everyone becomes agent Smith. Journalists have failed the public and would more appropriately be called billionaire PR agents because that's what they are. Our news reporters read scripts like robots. If they ever do try to question the validity of a news story on air, they get fired.

News reporters do damage control for billionaires. Then the American public foots the bill like a bunch of obedient dogs. Does that sound about right? How many politicians have been removed on the spot, stripped of their wealth and forced to work alongside their dejected voters for $10 an hour? It's time that disgraceful people experience a fall from grace. Why on earth should any of these guys fear doing harm to the group when none of us ever holds them accountable? We can change this.

We've been trained to attack and ridicule anyone proposing a theory about a possible truth that's been concealed by wealthy people that now own all of the TV networks. Nothing would unite the American people more than coming together and overturning the momentous lie of 911. It's been used to lead us into war under false pretenses. The truth can unite while lies untie our common bonds.

We all got manipulated by our TV sets on the morning of September 11th 2001. Only a very small percentage of the psyches (in a country full of not-so-bright people) have allowed our officials' version of the story to be challenged at all. In light of the damning evidence that does exist, it's now time for this to change. Public opinion about 911 is beginning to change (contrary to what you're being told by your TV).

Do you want to be one of the last zombies to finally discover the truth? I don't, and I'm willing to be ridiculed for proposing alternative explanations that are far more logical than George W Bush and President Obama's consensus of reality. Half of the country thinks that everything coming out of both of their mouths is a total lie, yet both Presidents back the same story.

Imagine that the tables are turned and it's the year 2000. Saddam Hussein is reading a children's book to a classroom full of kids inside an Iraqi elementary school. Right then, one of the tallest buildings in his capital city gets struck by a full-sized airliner during peacetime. Within minutes of the event, one of Mr. Hussein's security detail whispers into his ear to inform him of the crash. Because reading to a room full of innocent kids is great PR, cameras are on Mr. Hussein when he gets first word of the disaster. Instead of immediately excusing himself and leaving the room, Mr. Hussein continues on reading to the classroom of kids for another ten minutes. Within hours, Iraqi TV stations are reporting that American Terrorists are believed to be responsible for the attacks. Minimum civilian casualties are suffered in spite of two full-sized

Iraqi skyscrapers being demolished on camera. Eight years after declaring a retaliatory war on allies of the alleged attackers, there are 500,000 Americans dead. Bush did the exact same thing reading on for 10 minutes after first word of the plane strike. It made no sense. There's a reason that Mark Cuban was willing to invest millions of dollars to put "Loose Change" into theatres. We all know the kind of bets that rich people make. They only bet on…

The thing about truly demoralized victims is, even in the light of overwhelming evidence they'll continue to side with their oppressors. This is what's already happened to the same American public that we saw featured on "Jay Walking." Somehow we're allowing them (the idiotic public) to police us. The idiot masses have become so well-trained to defend the politicians' lies that honest people dare not speak the truth in public. Now you know why Orwell created Winston in "1984." The dead (brain dead) always attack the living, just like in every zombie movie ever made.

This point was very smugly made by former KGB agent Yuri Bezmenov when explaining how Russia had demoralized its people. Stalin took full control of a super power-sized country. The citizens were trained to police each other while criminals ran the economy into the ground (and millions of people slowly wasted away). You can bet that most of the Russian people thought that things were going just fine during that fiasco. The same can be said about the U.S. today. The majority of citizens likely mocked the intellectuals (critical thinkers) for trying to reason with them. As a country becomes more demoralized, drug and alcohol use go up.

The critical thinkers in pre-communist Russia failed to break through Stalin's mind control. They later got shipped out of the country after the takeover was complete. After all, you can't have brave, reasonable, and logical people hanging around a bunch of defeated human beings (undoing years of careful programming). If you don't realize that the American public has been systematically and scientifically conditioned to act as the government's watch dogs, (thought police) then you're likely one of them. That spell is being broken. For me, it's a matter of waking people up, or ending up in Siberia (Canada).

We've become a country full of addicts that must conform to the televised version of reality. Otherwise, we get attacked by our abused and indoctrinated neighbors that aren't ready to end the relationship yet. They don't have the guts to confront the real issues that keep them from escaping their own abusive lives. Instead, they drink, eat constantly, pop pills, or get high daily. If a completely invasive and all-controlling technological surveillance state (with cameras included) wasn't nearing completion (right in front of our eyes) then we'd have no problem with our neighbors doing a little partying. The problem is that the party has become non-stop for our beat-down comrades. Many Americans have become comfortably poor while their lives turn to crap. Pot is Soma from Brave New World. Its strength and popularity compared to just 30 years ago have grown exponentially. But, it's hard to be alarmed when everyone's on Soma.

Once we take the chemical escape the result is always the same, let somebody else deal with it. As a result, the whole group suffers due to abundant sources of cheap (slave-like) labor that doesn't demand respect. Reasonable people that won't replace God with worship of the government become less and less accepted by their indoctrinated neighbors. This is already happening in America. Government checks are now trumping self-sufficiency.

It's time to face the truth that we were conned on 911 to support billionaires' oil rights. There was a pre-existing long-term military strategy as in, "The Project for the New American Century." Please Google it and see what you find. Understand that in 1997 this think tank was formed in Washington D.C. to lay out future plans to ensure world dominance for the next one hundred years. The plan involved overthrowing multiple Middle-Eastern governments and also installing increased controls on the American people. This was all drawn up before 911 took place.

We aren't just going to send our children off to war to line the pockets of billionaires for no reason. An enemy attack on our soil makes sending our kids off to war a lot easier for all of us to feel good about. I'm sure you're aware that Dick Cheney and his former employer Halliburton made billions of dollars after 911 took place.

We were all lied to about the true perpetrators of 911. Just like in Hitler's Germany and in Stalin's Russia, it's all fun and games until your neighbor's eyes become filled with rage when you attempt to explain the truth to them. Learning how to talk about these subjects in public without getting yelled at is an art form that takes years to develop. Did both Stalin and Hitler rely on the idiot mob to keep the brightest and most loving citizens silent? The same has been done in America regarding 911.

Before 911, the American people didn't allow our phones to be tapped or ourselves to be treated as suspects every time that we wanted to get on an airplane. There's a very interesting film online called, "Invisible Empire" relating to this topic. We all understand that super wealthy men may become hell-bent on controlling the course of history. There are control freaks in this world, lots actually. Is it possible that they would rig the game in order to make themselves wealthy beyond our wildest dreams?

We all know that these types of people do exist and often seek positions of power. Is it possible that people involved with our political world would allow an attack and then blame it on one of their proposed targets? Do scammers exist? We've all crossed paths with liars and cheats during the course of our lives. We either choose to continue being their victims, or stand up to them and confront their lies. The reason that we don't do this very often is that we're afraid of the confrontation.

We'd rather lie to ourselves daily than be in a necessary confrontation with the unethical people that are bullying us. We do anything to avoid discomfort, especially when the uncomfortable action is the honorable one. If we want to regain some freedoms in America then we're going to have to force some uncomfortable confrontations with the shady people that have taken over our country.

Have I ever shown up and knocked on the front door of a person that ripped me off? Yes. They respond as any little kid does, with fear and anger. Have I survived the confrontations? Yes. I've also maintained my dignity and self-respect (two things that most Americans have long ago lost). We can all get it back by standing up for ourselves. Criminals are cowards and the public has been hypnotized by TV to believe the exact opposite. Let's force shady people to lash out at us for confronting them with the truth. This is much more honorable than silently sliding into the tyranny of Orwell's nightmares.

If we want to live in a free country where good people are in charge, then some unpopular conversations have to take place in many of our lives. We need to knock on our oppressors front doors, stare them in the faces, and confront them with the truth. Posting things on Facebook is a masturbatory effort. It fails to address bad behaviors face to face.

Stare evil in the face and speak the truth. Evil will most often run out of the room or dismiss us from their lives. After the confrontation is over, we cease to have an ongoing relationship with an asshole. The universe rewards true bravery and personal courage with both immediate and future freedoms. We shouldn't believe that groveling to unethical people is the best course of action. Staying surrounded by hopeless co-workers will only be rewarded with a lifetime of miserable servitude. Not to God, but to white-collar criminals that only pretend to believe in God. People's actions show whether or not they believe at all.

We all need to renegotiate our lives in an active effort to create mutually beneficial relationships. We need to walk away from those that only take our energy. The win-lose sociopaths of our society can run out of victims and go out of business. A less-rigged market and the American public can do all of this. The general public does have the power to take down corrupt leaders and dismantle the rackets that they've created.

Chapter 4 – Indoctrinated Americans

Anyone that believes in the Republican vs. Democrat paradigm is currently part of the billionaires' zombie army. If you truly want out of the matrix, then you'll have to fully unplug yourself as described in this book. The results will be shocking. Our loving elites at the top of the pyramid are used to having open doors everywhere they go. Perhaps it's time that this begins to happen for you too. It's going to take some work, but the benefits will be worth it.

Millions of Russian citizens walked around believing that Stalin was the good guy. The same went for Adolf Hitler in the eyes of the German beer-drinking people. If those guys hadn't successfully programmed the public to follow their lead, then the people never would've participated in a superpower of the dictators' making, but they did. We're no less at risk of being programmed ourselves.

The Germans weren't stupid, but they sure did drink often and got into amphetamine during Hitler's rise. What about the Russians? If you became aware that someone has hacked into your head and has been controlling your actions, wouldn't you want to cut the connection? Most of us would. I'm proposing that there's a possible way to do so.

Zombie Americans that simply repeat the Republican or Democrat talking points are still buying the magician's trick. Believing that Democrat or Republican makes any difference at all pretty much confirms that you're running on TV programming. Democrats blame Republicans and vice versa leaving the billionaire architects of all public policy untouched. More than half of the public is completely dissatisfied with our government all of the time. These are all pre-determined policies that can only be rammed through while citizens make up excuses for their own party's actions. Can't the same be said in all dictatorships worldwide?

Zbigniew Brzezinski is one of the brains behind Obama's TV character. Men like Mr. Brzezinski and Henry Kissenger are just a few of the major players that have steered our society in the direction that we're now going. In fact, they're so cocky and believe that the public is so stupid that they've written books announcing their exact plans. This is fact, and you can read their books. They do exist. Radio host Alex Jones frequently makes this point (to his now massive audience).

If you really don't get that the ownership class looks down upon the public as a bunch of programmable pawns, then you're mistaken. The guys in office actually get-off on how badly they can lie to us without us even noticing. These are the type of people that are only happy if they're getting away with something. Haven't you ever met someone that was always attempting to better their position no matter how good they had it? These are Win-Lose negotiators and they're currently dominating our planet. These architects of our society will continue asserting more control over the public for as long as we allow it. Nothing shy of complete global control and world domination will satisfy them.

We can't allow people like this to continue selling us on the idea that we need more and more police and surveillance everywhere. Otherwise, we'll be living in a completely controlled society with no freedoms at all. The next big goal is to have troops on our streets and have the public welcome it. How could the current rulers accomplish this?

The same sociopaths that want troops on our streets would allow attacks on American soil and then insist that martial law is needed. Why? They don't want you getting lippy when they dissolve your 401k account and cut Social Security benefits in half in the very near future. It's not that the checks will get smaller, it's that the dollars will purchase 50 percent less stuff. Have you eaten meat or shaved lately? There has also been a well-organized effort by the mainstream media to pour gasoline on pre-existing racial tensions. Race riots nationwide would also open the gates to having troops on our streets (just like in all dictatorships worldwide). Once troops are installed, they're a real bitch to get rid of.

Greece has called a similar rapid economic decline in its citizen's lives, austerity measures. The U.S. has chosen to use Gas-

Lighting on its not-so-bright citizenry. Gas-Lighting is where you tell somebody that everything is going just fine while standing in front of their burning-down house. Treat sane observers as if they're crazy while patting their stupefied neighbors on the head. Political Correctness.

Telling the American public that there's a 6% unemployment rate in 2015 via all major media outlets is a prime example of this. In reality, millions of previously employed people have given up looking for work and now live at home with their parents (who get a government check). A few million of these people are now completely omitted from the measurement process. What the public sees and hears on TV is propaganda. TV in America has become the Ministry of Truth. 6% nationwide unemployment, that's double-plus good!

Detroit slashed its peoples' retirement benefits recently due to bankruptcy and nothing happened. Much of Detroit already looks like a dilapidated war zone. Don't you get that the federal government is also going bankrupt right now? Other entire countries are also on the verge of going broke, like Greece. Have you heard about Homeland Security purchasing 1.6 billion rounds of hollow point bullets? Sounds like zombie ammo to me. Seven billion people must find a way to stop a few thousand elites from hoarding all of the world's resources (while holding guns to the rest of our heads).

Millions of Americans should have been out in the streets the day that our Supreme Court ruled that a corporation was equal to a person, but we weren't. Those corporations can now contribute unlimited funds to any candidate without public disclosure. In January of 2010 our government officially told us all that corporations can now legally buy any election. Go vote, it really really counts. A lot. Unless criminals are in charge and put their people in place to count the votes.

There were limits that protected the American people from being outspent in political campaigns by mega-powerful corporations. This is one of the most ludicrous rule changes imposed on the super-high public after the post 911 apocalypse. We once had a framework of freedom and protections against tyranny known as our Constitution. It only works in a country that has citizens with working brains, hearts, and some courage. Do you presently see a smart, honest, and courageous public?

Avoiding the staggering percentage of demoralized Americans by shopping at Target won't stop an army of nanny-state Americans from repeating what was already done in Nazi Germany, Socialist Russia, or in Communist China. It could happen here (and is). There's now a massive population of demoralized Americans. Who is it that's going to successfully pull their strings?

Clearly our Constitution states that our elected officials must obey the will of the people. Are they? We all know the answer but we're all too afraid to confront the con-men that keep ripping us all off. We're now being controlled by profit making machines rather than by rational people that care about our group's well being. I'm not comforted when the Walgreen's workers tell me to, "Be well" just like the disarmed and spineless future Americans featured in Sly Stallone's "Demolition Man." Try going to Redbox for that movie, it's not there.

If you want to help America, then start by changing yourself in a way that boosts your own level of confidence first. The directions on how to unplug from the control system are very straight forward and you have the freewill to choose. The controllers think that you're too well-trained and too hypnotized to walk over to your cable box and unplug it. I know differently.

People that have successfully unplugged from the programming end up with less fear, less anger, more energy, and a greater spiritual connection. Not church people spirituality and not pill-bottle spirituality, but something that strangers will see and will want. Once your own consciousness has been boosted, others will begin to want what you have. This is how we save America.

We must empower ourselves first. If we continue refusing to change ourselves for the better first, then a minority of super greedy people will continue dictating a lower quality of life to a bunch of hypnotized zombies. That zombie army will be ordered to eliminate people with brains and resources one day. Stupid people can be trained to do anything. Because of this, stupid Americans are an important issue that you, I, and everybody else should be concerned about. These are valuable people that can be unplugged from their TV programming, weaned off of their drinking and drug habits and brought back to full consciousness again. It can be done. We need them on our team, not the dictator's.

What do you think Nazi Germany was like for the wealthy Jewish people right before things got really bad? Are you really telling me that all 50 million Americans on food stamps are fully conscious, physically fit, and mentally healthy people? How about we all demand drug testing for food stamps? This kind of logical change is something that the majority of hard working Americans would likely support.

We must face the underlying issues that have created a country full of self-pity-filled victims. Those were exactly the drunken German and Russian people that were handed sharp looking uniforms and used to carry out anything that their government told them to do. What do you think that the TSA is becoming?

There's literally an army of TSA and Homeland Security agents that are heavily armed (tanks included). There are videos of trains shipping tanks across the U.S. during the last few years. What do you think the average IQ is for all of these new Homeland Security agents? How many of them are on delusional power trips and will do anything that they're ordered to do? Of these newly employed TSA and Homeland Security agents, how many do you think have drinking and drug habits?

How many of Hitler's Nazis do you think had drinking and drug habits too? The German economy had been horrible for ten years before moronic citizens would do anything for a high wage and a sharp uniform. What will drug addicts and alcoholics do in order to continue funding their habits and feeding their families? What percentage of Americans would now qualify as prescription drug addicts or functioning alcoholics? Of the people that do firmly fall into that category, how many are now members of the working-poor? Do you really understand exactly how far along our country has been taken in a socialist direction? Collectively, our country is like a loud-mouthed drunken fat man that's about to get knocked out.

Our politicians and billionaires have been outmaneuvering the public for decades. If you want vampire speed then you've got to stop following the slow zombie diet. Stop getting outrun by faster people with working brains. If you like the idea of a more powerful processer in your own head and a better body that results from more movement, then I'm telling you of a possible way to achieve it. If we weren't being outsmarted by these people then only a few of them wouldn't be in charge of all of us, but they are.

If we had more intelligence, then rich politicians on TV would no longer be dictating directions to us. The same could be said for the police that are just as TV-programmed to protect rich sociopaths while pepper-spraying average citizens for speaking the truth. Most police are good people with good intentions. If all police completely stopped watching TV and refused the slow zombie diet, then they too would realize that they're being used to protect evil men (and are completely expendable).

The mainstream media has been fanning the flames of racial division causing public attacks on police officers. There are lots of good cops out there being put in harm's way by divide and conquer TV programming. The actual number of Baltimore, Maryland cops killed in 2015 has eluded national TV coverage. A more controlling and more oppressive replacement system will be rolled out if unsuspecting Americans take the bait. An army of Americans is now dependent upon monthly government checks. If race riots do occur in America, then troops on our streets can be rolled out and food stamp recipients will be the last to protest. Give a man something and you gain power over him. It's not at all fun being owned.

When picturing food stamp people do you picture someone that's physically fit, quick-witted, and spreading joy wherever they go? Do you think most of these people believe that they create their own destiny or are victims of circumstance? We all know the truthful answers. How many hours a day of TV do you think food-stamp zombies are watching? If you don't like this happening, then start unplugging them.

I'm sure that being a drug addict has no effect on somebody's level of hopefulness or their ability to solve problems and put in an honest day's work. At some point an insane person is faced with the premise that they've lost their sanity. If you've completely lost control of your drinking or use constant pills to feel normal; then at some level you've lost control of your mind. If this wasn't the truth, then you wouldn't need the daily drinks or pill sedation to deal with reality.

Unemployed Americans don't realize that it's their TV that has created the present belief systems in their heads. If your present belief system has you sitting at home unemployed and feeling sorry for yourself, then it's time to unplug the cable box. By doing this you can begin to install new beliefs into your new operating system. This change will produce a healthier you with a more powerful brain. This new belief system will actually begin to solve your problems.

The new brain power unleashed will allow you to out-compete TV-hypnotized zombies. Your brain and body will operate like a virus free computer system, fast. If you want a faster processor that allows you to create a better body, then refuse average American amounts of TV programming. The politicians from both parties can't lie to you if you aren't watching them. Does that make sense? This is how you begin to regain control of your life. Your own freewill is being restored at this very moment. This book does boost self-control and has already helped others before you to break free from hellish situations. This is fact.

Whether we vote Republican or Democrat, the minority of super wealthy will continue to simply tell the President what to tell the zombies. As long as we're all tuned in to our TVs, we the zombies will slowly move in the desired direction. To pretend that half brain-dead people aren't littered all over the place is to deny the slow-moving and bloated people that you see every day in any grocery store. How on earth could the whole scam be ended by something as simple as everyone unplugging their TVs for an entire month?

George Carlin did a stand-up routine that clearly pointed out the obvious sham of our political system. Mr. Carlin wasn't afraid to speak truth regarding the true ownership of not only the current political system, but billionaires' common belief that they own you. I think a quick YouTube search of George Carlin and the words, "They own you" ought to do it.

How many times has the public voted one party out of office only to have things get even worse when the new leadership takes charge? It's like we all have a big bully that asks us if we'd like to be punched in the face or punched in the stomach. Either way, we're all getting punched and having our lunch money stolen by a group of frat boys in expensive suits. No matter who wins, half of the country is totally pissed-off by it. The other half that did win then gets double-crossed by their own party. This same process has repeated for my entire lifetime. This is the truth.

Of course the winning team (losing tax-base) is too proud to admit that their candidate completely abandoned all promises after being elected (marks). This process repeats for both parties and their supporters. There are a handful of extra dizzy marks called "Swing voters." My loving parents fall into this category. They trust people too much, and as a result continue to get conned by actual sociopaths in their immediate life. As far as wicked people see it, a lack of discernment is the fault of a mark. Boosting the public's ability to discern draws attacks from the wicked. In order for people like my parents to stop getting conned, this sounds fair to me.

We're like an entire country of married people that have an openly cheating spouse. We all stay silent because we're still in a big house in a nice neighborhood. We fear that we might end up living in a much worse place. So, we pop those pills or have those drinks that keep our consciences quiet. As the economy has declined, peoples' moral compasses have followed. Really, we've lost respect for ourselves and our cheating politicians know it (and love it). Cheating has never been so easy for them. The 60 inch TVs, weed, and feel-good prescription pills have made us easy marks. If there's one thing that screw-up rich kids love, it's a rigged game that they can't lose.

A bunch of mentally impaired adults keep on going along with a con-game that only less-than-average people would buy into. Please YouTube the following video that explains how we've let things get so bad without even noticing: KGB Bezmenov 1985 - Four Steps to Subversion of a Nation. Listen to the smugness of the man explaining how it works (because he knows that it will work again). It did.

The children of tyrants and known criminals don't deserve to control the rest of us with stolen wealth. As a group, we must come to grips that these same royal bloodlines have used television to perpetuate the very belief that they're more important than the rest of us. They're not. They're just people and are equally as fallible, flawed and unimportant to the universe as the rest of us. We're all human beings having a human experience. Don't be tricked into surrendering all of your power to them.

If the actual TV programming didn't paint the picture of just how powerful they are, (and how powerless we are) then maybe we'd figure out that it's all an illusion. Millions and billions of us have vastly more power than only a few thousand elite worldwide. They only rule over the masses with perceived power. When 7 billion people decide that a new way of life is needed, it'll happen.

If Aliens were to show up on earth today and we attempted to tell them that we're a vastly intelligent and highly evolved species of which billions suffered (while a few thousand of equal intelligence and strength ruled over the rest of us) they would laugh in our faces! Most Americans have an ego that will defend their slave masters at the previous statement. After all, we've been subjected to a lifetime of conditioning (like dogs) to defend our masters (no matter how poor we're getting). It's as if we're suffering ant farms all over the world lacking the basic intelligence to remove a few bad ants. Here we are, billions of us waiting for the thumb of God to smash a few bad ants (failing to comprehend that we are the thumb).

How are living conditions for a billion people living in communist China right now? Have you tried thinking your way out of a paper bag when rice is all that you can afford to eat every day? Diets that are void of fats and proteins destroy brain power. The most oppressed populations on earth are held down not only by religious programming and brute force, but by their diets as well.

India also has hundreds of millions of people living in complete poverty right now. Just like a billion dirt-poor Chinese people (that worship their government), the poverty-stricken Indian people have very little meat and fat in their diets. What's happened to the price of meat in America since 2008? Cattle farmers across America have faced a tidal wave of government regulations that have driven up the cost of beef. Rest assured, the elites eat meat and plenty of it. Poor people worldwide are steered into diets that destroy brain power. Meats become an upper-class privilege while alcohol stays amazingly affordable (in spite of food inflation).

Americans back in the 1950's were frequently eating burgers and drinking milkshakes (and they weren't getting fat). I don't know about you but I'm going to avoid sharing a similar diet to the most oppressed people on earth. Find out what types of foods prosperous people are actually eating, and copy them. We do worship Pro athletes, right? What kind of diets do they have? Do as successful people do and try not to copy entire countries of slaves. Don't forget, soy protein mimics estrogen; American men that want to stay masculine should avoid it.

If there is some sort of spiritual realm beyond our sight, isn't it possible that higher intelligences would attempt to reveal the control system? Our discovery of new ideas has improved our quality of life throughout recorded history. Do you really think that the current controllers of the masses would be eager to let go? Do abusive spouses easily let go? The good news is that humanity far outnumbers the few bad eggs that have been abusing our group. One by one, people worldwide can begin strengthening themselves and regaining rights. Good people on earth far outnumber the bad.

The public has been carefully trained to ridicule new ideas that could teach them how to turn off the wizard's movie projector.

A few really greedy billionaires have created an army of idiots (not you of course) to do their bidding. The elites don't care if they destroy the middle class and the millionaires that helped in making America a pleasant place to live.

History channel recently produced lengthy documentaries about Hitler's rise to power and the poor economic conditions prior to Germany's socialist takeover. Hitler and the other Nazi leaders were extremely interested in the use of propaganda. The Nazis proved that huge groups of previously normal people could be manipulated to do just about anything by a tiny number of clever people.

Millionaires need to start identifying and unplugging average people from the main source of propaganda (TV) before history repeats itself. We're much closer to full blown tyranny with troops on our streets than the public realizes. Nearly 1/3 of the U.S. population is currently dependent on government checks. That's 100 million people that would likely stay home and stay quiet even if troops were added to our streets. Becoming aware that such a possibility even exists then prevents it from happening.

The German people that became Nazis didn't go on to do all of those terrible things because it was their childhood dream; they were skillfully manipulated by others to act out terrible behaviors. Hitler proved beyond the shadow of a doubt that the human mind can easily be programmed to do anything. Regardless of how selfish and destructive the master is, when people are fed the right formula of beliefs, they'll then act accordingly. Do you think that TSA agents patting down little kids with clean cut middle-class parents is a normal behavior?

We're being conditioned to feel like inmates while the additional cameras, guards, and rules are being constructed right in front of us all. The right to choose your own child's school lunch is being taken away in America. We celebrate a holiday called Independence Day and at the same time our government is attempting to dictate the diets of millions of non-prison inmates. The public must push back now or more rights will be lost.

Hitler and his high ranking SS officers spoke about the use of propaganda. They said things like, "Even if we tell a lie, if we say it enough times it becomes the truth." How many times have we caught our own politicians doing the same thing? When exactly are we going to face the truth that we've been in an abusive relationship with sociopaths in suits?

How many married people do you know that only stay due to low self-respect or more appropriately, fear? It's never comfortable or easy to end serious relationships. However, the benefits and self-respect that go along with doing the right thing are well worth the short-term pain and discomfort. It's much better to be in pain for weeks or months than to remain a victim for a lifetime. We only have ourselves to blame when "stuck" in these bad situations (due to our own lack of personal courage).

I remember seeing a bumper sticker on a beat-up late model Oldsmobile that said, "Stuck in Cleveland" just before I left town. I told everyone around me in that hopeless city that I was going on a 1000 mile journey to a better job market. All of the oppressed Clevelanders (low-income majority) quickly justified to me why they couldn't do the same. Over and over again people said that I was lucky, and then immediately hurled an excuse that cemented them in their bad situations for life. It was like the land of a thousand excuses.

One of the most successful and charismatic managers that I've ever worked for once said, "The world is full of two types of people, excusers and producers." Look around at the conditions of a city and you'll quickly know who you're surrounded by. Millions of Americans keep running back to the comfort of the bottle because they're too afraid to face the truth regarding their own lousy job, spouse, or self. It's now time that this changes.

It's time for us to stand up for ourselves as a united people with common interests at stake. How we treat others and our own level of bravery or cowardliness is directly reflected back at us over the course of a lifetime. Short term events both good and bad do take place, but our reaction to these events and our choices thereafter are what determine our destiny. We must accept that we're building our own reality one decision at a time.

Those living in corrupt areas where the majority of people act completely selfish won't get positive feedback for positive behaviors. The positive action in that scenario is to walk away when you're badly outnumbered by demoralized people. Not all battles on all fronts can be won. If you find yourself surrounded by miserable people that all seem to be experiencing hellish situations, then you may be living in a hellhole. If you come to believe that you don't deserve to be in hell for any longer, then leave.

Breaking through years of brilliantly orchestrated mind control via television isn't an easy task but it's happening right now. Walls in your mind constructed by sociopaths are being demolished at a rapid pace. Once somebody's willing to listen, we can then shine a light on when, where and why our country was lied to on a massive scale. We may have all been conned on 911 by a handful of corrupt people to behave in a way that they desired.

False Flag attacks have been used by governments and by kings throughout recorded history in order to sway public opinion. These attacks directly benefit the perpetrator of the staged event while blaming the attack on a proposed target. This is perhaps one of the darkest sides of human history that we must face in order to empower ourselves.

Pretending that no monsters have infiltrated our own government is just as ridiculous as pretending that no monsters infiltrated our most sacred and holy of places. If evil sick men were able to hide in the Catholic Church and dress up as holy men, then they could certainly hide in the shady world of politics. Clearly man has demonstrated that a small percentage of sick people will pursue honorable positions (and steal easy meals).

God-fearing people need to stop projecting their own consciences onto a small group of men that have none left. Humanity is greatly guilty of this fatal mistake. We keep on projecting our sense of right and wrong onto the criminal politicians and bankers that are feeding off of us. It's time that this comes to an end because we all deserve better than this.

If Hitler and the Nazis successfully pulled-off such a stunt against the German people then it's very plausible that it could be done again. Don't we sometimes refer to German engineering when speaking of the best and the brightest? Surely you'd have a hard time arguing that German scientists weren't considered to be smart. We now know that Nazi scientists were brought to the US after World War II had ended. They were brought here to help us to compete against the Russians.

NASA and the United States space program was headed up by an ex-Nazi scientist named Wernher von Braun. This is a fact, and the American public should be fully aware of Project Paperclip. The German people that got conned by Hitler's False Flag attack (using the Reichstag Fire which swayed public opinion toward Hitler's secret agenda) weren't dummies. However, the con did work. The American people aren't all dummies either, but it's entirely possible that we too were conned on 911. This possibility really sucks, but that doesn't eliminate its ability to exist.

A famous speaker named David Icke has recently coined the phrase "Problem, Reaction, Solution" to describe exactly how corrupted officials can use staged terror attacks to sway public opinion in any direction that they desire. No, none of us would ever do such a thing, but most of us also wouldn't run for political office either. We all seem to acknowledge that the political world is full of snakes. None of us normal people would do any of this, but we've witnessed bad people in good positions throughout our lives. It does happen.

The rest of us that do have consciences must now force dishonest men's lies out into the light. It may cost us our lives, but as David Icke says, "The truth is like a lion, once it's been let out of its cage nobody has to defend it, it will defend itself." It's painfully simple to understand how False Flags are used. There are strong implications that the Gulf of Tonkin incident was also a False Flag operation used by the US government to justify Vietnam. This is a huge deal but is completely missing from the data files in most American zombie brains. The American people need a good reason to be willing to send their own kids off to war.

Barring an attack, selling the American public on the idea that a few wealthy men will get a lot wealthier wouldn't be enough to justify war. We won't risk the lives of our own lower and middle-class kids if our emotions haven't been stirred up sufficiently. That's where the False Flag operation comes in handy for our loving slave masters, I mean politicians to use on us all. War has been used to grab cheap resources from foreign countries (for the benefit of the super wealthy only) for thousands of years. Things haven't changed very much.

If we're all told that we were attacked by terrorists from a foreign country (that just so happens to have something our owners want) then we're all for it! I don't want to be a rube, but I certainly can admit that I've been duped into supporting wars as seen on TV. I remember watching Desert Storm and cheering against Saddam Hussein. What most people don't know is that our U.S. government had funded and backed Mr. Hussein and only later double-crossed him.

The public acts as if there are no politicians capable of this when dismissing 911 claims. As far as my lifetime has taught me, rich men wearing suits are capable of anything. There are both good and bad people that exist across all walks of life. Evil is a strong closer. No matter how far-fetched the too-good to be true deal offered to the marks (public) may be; they seem to go for it.

When we come across extremely intelligent individuals that happen to understand how many things work, we often refer to them as bright. Bright people can learn many new things, retain information, and then solve a huge variety of problems with ease compared to slow-moving Walmart zombies demanding welfare checks. As with every other deal with the devil, the welfare recipients will gradually be forced to support full-blown tyranny and will later be put to work. Too good to be true does not exist.

We must work hard if we expect to be rewarded accordingly. Do you think that a slow-moving and bloated Walmart zombie (sadly rolling past you in their scooter chair of sadness) has laid out this set of revelations for you? Do you believe that they are pro-government handout for the rest of their lifetime or not? Do you want to work 50 hours per week (for the rest of your lifetime) to support "disabled" fat people?

Those same people receiving monthly get-out-of-work-free checks are about to start voting away all of our freedoms at a rapid pace. They wouldn't hesitate to vote Constitutionalists and any non-party members to be sent straight off to the FEMA camps in order to keep that magic disability check. What would the angels say about welfare cheats? What if we aren't the top beings in the universe or even here on earth?

If a corrupt government gets taken apart by honest people, then all of those that are cheating the system will lose their free meal tickets. So, the least healthy and the least honest will be the strongest resistance to the truth. There are appropriate times to defend ourselves when people around us behave like assholes. Remember, a country full of dependants all sharing a victim mentality will rigorously defend a dictatorship.

Is it possible that the elites have successfully placed walls between average Americans and increased intelligence? What if the people at the very tippy top of the financial pyramid referred to the people at the bottom as the walking dead? People all over the world have been oppressed with a steady diet of fear, stress, drugs, and alcohol. All sold to us in large by what we've been told is entertainment on our TVs. Those of us operating at this spiritual minimum are indeed referred to as, "The walking dead" by upper-level Free Masons. Do you get the tremendously ironic joke about one of America's most popular TV series? We're actually watching a show about ourselves in the eyes of the "enlightened" ones that own everything. We're like a big herd of cattle that loves watching a TV show about only slightly less healthy cows getting shot in the head for an hour each week. Mooooooooh!

Why do zombie Americans also seem to love watching other desperate people get ripped-off on History Channel all day long? Seriously, why are fat tattooed takers (that shear people all day and wear sun glasses indoors) on our History Channel? Maybe it's to document the historical account of how decent Americans stood by (like cattle) while tattooed pieces of crap (that completely lack a conscience) have stepped into the new management class of America. This is the televised liquidation of fallen American assets.

Whenever there's a bunch of drunks and drug addicts living in a particular part of a city, what types of stores start popping up on every street corner? Did it ever occur to you that your favorite TV show may really just be a zombie training video for defeated Americans? It's to prepare you not to be afraid of the fat tattooed man wearing all black at your local shearing station. These shows are humanizing the parasitic people that are about to man-handle you. These TV shows are zombie training videos. You can turn off the training whenever you want. Just unplug your TV and stop doing what the other defeated people are doing. You're no longer a victim and your luck is improving.

Masonic Lodges appear in cities and suburbs throughout the country. They're associated with the Free Masons and illuminati that anyone attempting to talk about was ridiculed for until recently. In the Masonic lodges individuals that work their way up the scale of enlightenment also refer to spiritually unaware people as dogs. Checkerboard floors are also a symbol that pokes fun at the ignorant public. The checker board pattern infers that we're pawns being controlled on somebody else's chess board. The black and white squares also represent duality. The ignorant public sees everything in black or white, right or wrong, Democrat or Republican. The enlightened elites aren't bound by these same rules and most frequently function in the grey area (that only high-powered lawyers can protect you in). Voters remain poor, and Masons continue networking.

Do you want to be somebody else's pawn? The Internet and even the History Channel have opened up the flood gates regarding the existence of secret societies controlling vast wealth in the US. Also note that our troops that are on the front lines (for the elites' profits and protection) wear dog tags. Many troops then return home and become cops. Become fully conscious to avoid becoming a German shepherd serving a socialist state.

There are plenty of God-fearing and well-intentioned people that belong to secret societies. The majority of their members are at lower ranks much like people at the bottom of a corporation. Most Free Masons have no idea what the people at the top are actually up to. Low-level Masons are misinformed of what the people at the top of the organization are ritualistically worshipping, Lucifer. Yup, you read that right. The top level Masons worship Lucifer, an angel of light according to them and Scottish Right Free Mason founder, Albert Pike.

A very infamous character named Aleister Crowley happened to be a 33rd degree Free Mason and had heavy occult ties. Many celebrities where t-shirts paying tribute to this occult leader. History Channel has a series called Brad Meltzer's Decoded that actually proved that the Statue of Liberty is a Masonic symbol that portrays Lucifer, the angel of light. Do you get why the Masonic lodges all over the United States don't talk about what it is that they're worshipping? Do as thou wilt, that's how they live.

The Free Masons and the illuminati have kept their societies secret from public awareness for hundreds of years. George W. Bush and John Kerry are recent high-level officials that belong to the Skull and Bones Society (Illuminati) at Yale University. During the 2004 Presidential election a college student was tazed on camera for daring to ask John Kerry about his Skull and Bones membership. It turns out that many Presidents and politicians are members of this secret good-ole-boy network that also just so happens to practice occult rituals (just like Hitler and the Nazis also did). Once again, twenty years ago nobody would have accepted that tons of priests around the world were molesting altar boys, but molest they did.

The rich scumbag network's been sneaking around for way too long. Let's start shining some light into clubs with secret handshakes. We're grown adults and we can handle this. These guys aren't having bake sales to raise money for new bowling shirts. They worship a different God than the rest of us do, and it's not a God that allows for a strong conscience (or any at all). They will not protect us.

We're talking about wealthy men practicing dark rituals and requesting help from negative entities (not God) to aid them in dominating the rest of us. They really believe in this stuff and we keep allowing them to make decisions for our group. Good people that believe in God need to remove these men from power now. When we actually started finding out that priests were molesting children, we investigated, found the hidden truth and booted them out. It's now time that the same is done for devil-worshipping rich dudes that incredibly, do exist.

Wealthy men in these secret societies have kept this stuff secret for a reason. Generally, when people are doing something really good for their group, their ego wants to receive praise. We all want to gain acceptance from the group we belong to. Throughout our entire lifetime what type of deeds do we normally keep secret from the rest of the world?

If the Free Masons are up to good deeds that benefit all of mankind, then why don't they come out and show us all? I'm guessing because selfish and self-serving behaviors are taking place. Which option sounds more logical to you? It's about time that we turn off the 3 hour football game (excuse to get high or drunk) and start addressing the evil men that are threatening the future of our country. A full-blown Marxist-style takeover of America is well underway right now.

Ignorance isn't bliss. If there happens to be a rich guys' network that encourages them to behave without a conscience (other than corporate America), we ought to know about it. Watching TV for three hours a night and getting drunk 7 days per week isn't going to change anything for the better. We prefer knowing the truth, even if it turns out to be very ugly. Cows that never investigate what's on the other side of the fence deserve to be slaughtered (according to our leaders).

We're not supposed to be behaving like livestock (docile, dumb, and unaware that someone else sees us as nothing other than a source of energy). We've been pacified with booze, drugs, and a television that dominates 85% of the population's ability to reason. The top 15% of the brightest individuals are still able to critically think while watching TV and movies. The other 85% is toast after just a few minutes. Most of those Walmart zombies are toast and we know it. If they were offered the option to send millionaires off to re-education camps in exchange for more handouts and a chance to inherit their empty houses, they'd line up around the block to vote-away their perceived oppressors. It's been done before.

Our ego jumps up and says, "Oh that's me, I'm part of the 15% that's immune to TV's hypnotic effect!" Really? Have you always scored in the top 15% of your class? Have you ever met a really stupid person that was completely unaware of how truly stupid they were?

This is supposed to be the "ah hah" moment where if you didn't always score at the top of your class with ease and you're currently watching hours of TV per day, then you're likely one of the zombies. If you want to be free, then this is an excellent time to walk over to your cable box and unplug it. My mental chains were broken just as yours are being now. It does make a huge difference.

Chapter 5 – How To Increase Consciousness

Clearly our world has some individuals that worship money and power. Changing others violates their freewill and is usually a big damn waste of energy that always backfires. It makes more sense to focus on small things in our own lives. If there are super wealthy people that have become drunk with power, then their corrupted egos have justified to them that they're entitled to control the rest of us for as long as they're alive. We're going to have to save ourselves by acquiring knowledge and raising our own level of consciousness beyond the normal 85% of grocery store zombies.

What is consciousness? It's our level of awareness, perception, self-control, and the ability to assess a situation using our heart-based conscience (not fear). People at very high levels of consciousness are governed by a very large conscience making it nearly impossible to lie. They won't screw over their fellow man in order to benefit themselves because their conscience won't allow it. We do know people like this. We all know some people that are simply more honest than what's normal. They do exist and are highly unpopular during socialist takeovers.

To develop a truly high level of consciousness is to become an unselfish person, but not a doormat. How many of us feel completely overwhelmed and choose to hide in our homes and avoid the public as much as possible (unless buzzed, high, or pilled-up into confidence)? For really smart people, alcohol is the magic elixir that allows you to blend in with the 85%ers without them attacking the crime of too much thought. If you were completely sober and attempted to start reasoning with the sedated 85% ers, then you're likely going to get yelled at. This is why many older men and women in the former Soviet Union crawled into vodka bottles. It only took 80 years for Russia to turn back towards God after a complete economic collapse. There, in spite of smart people, socialism failed.

Our psychologically defeated neighbors are simply following their training (just like the German and Russian citizens once did). It did happen back then, and has happened in America since 911. We're not supposed to be sedating ourselves to accommodate hypnotized idiots that will attack anyone who violates their politician-approved TV programming. Not-give-a-shit in a can isn't proving to be a good nationwide solution to the American zombie (victim) epidemic. Our country has grown dumber, and at a rapid pace.

In oppressive places and in stressful situations, we naturally revert backward to our primal instincts. That's exactly what has happened in America following 911. When people get badly stressed out, they tend to act like primates that are mostly concerned with food, sex, and shelter. Corrupt government leaders know this and have used TV to inject a constant stream of fear into the public's heads. Most elderly Americans watch tons of TV and are extremely fearful citizens as a result. Please refer to Maslow's Hierarchy of Needs on the next page:

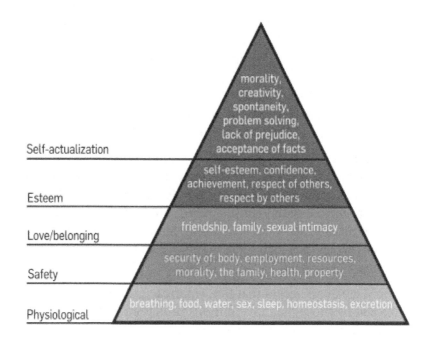

Out of 7 billion people on earth, how many do you think have achieved security of their own property, health, family, morality, and employment? Does our planet deserve a passing or a failing grade? Most people on earth spend lifetimes at the bottom.

If a super intelligent and spiritually gifted group of ETs landed on earth today, do you think they'd find humanity to be highly intelligent beings of logic, love and creativity, or hairless monkeys that just learned how to speak? The actual numbers at the bottom of the pyramid would more likely tip the scale toward monkeys that can talk. Isn't it about time that all of us walking dead started breaking through the walls put in place by assholes? Don't human beings deserve a fighting chance to experience safety, security, love, esteem, and self-actualization? Of course hard work, dedication, and consistent effort over the course of time will have to be put in. Do voters exist in dictatorships across this planet that put in all of the efforts but get none of the benefits?

The act of maintaining frequent sobriety from alcohol, weed, or pills is now a rejection of the control system that we live in. It's happening now and the world elites are panicking. Each next stunt to scare us all with is failing. Our politicians same old cons are becoming obvious to an awakening public. Establishment backed politicians are losing the popular vote to outsider candidates.

We can all accept that the American public is being outsmarted by those that have billions of dollars. Otherwise, the rest of us that do work all the time wouldn't be so damn broke, but we are. We deserve access to the same food, shelter, and feelings of safety and security as party members' children. They aren't superior beings. We didn't get born on earth to be dominated by people rigging the game. We're supposed to call out cheats and make life uncomfortable for them. It can be done.

If you're one of the working poor that allows richer sociopaths to treat you like a second-class citizen, (rather than demanding respect) then it's your own fault. The working-poor across this earth need to figure this out. There are way more of us of equal intelligence and strength that have the power to renegotiate wages, rents, and exactly who's making the rules. We all have power in this game.

A good exercise to change your perspective on the people all around you is to look at them as little more than monkeys that can talk. I'm not talking about you of course, but look at those Walmart shoppers and sports stadiums full of drunken screaming idiots as little more than hairless talking apes. We all agree that our country is overflowing with idiots.

We actually had a TV show called "Are You Smarter Than A Fifth Grader." Don't worry, when that fifth grader graduates high school, their prescribed adderall and military-grade weed habit (Project MK-Naomi) will have happily serving coffee while saving up for tattoos. We also saw "Jay Walking" featured on Jay Leno which showcased the absolute ignorance of the public. Our psyche chooses to laugh rather than cry at the sad truth that surrounds us every day.

If people were given the opportunity to bring down the walls between them and consciousness, they would. I'm talking about the 85%ers that we've all been conforming to. Political correctness in a criminally run society (given that most politicians are liars and cheats) is a losing strategy. We often have to be drunk or on pills just to tolerate the group we now belong to. It's time to leave behind old beliefs.

We can unplug ourselves from a system that only seeks to serve itself and is leaving average people in ruins. If this wasn't the truth, then 50 million Americans wouldn't be on food stamps. Who wants to be dependent on the same government that they have nothing but contempt for? If you're on food stamps and you don't like rich old white guys in expensive suits, (that belong to secret societies with secret handshakes) then please find a different owner to supply your daily meals.

Obama may be the spokesperson, but he's no different than the front desk worker at a hotel. The customers never get to see the real owner face to face. We all know that a bunch of billionaire old white guys own most of the world; Them, and a handful of tyrannical sheiks that forbid women from driving cars. The Presidents do what these billionaires tell them to. Our leaders seem to be acting out of fear. As a species evolves, the notion of royalty should become more and more absurd. If one royal monkey in the jungle attempted to starve an entire community, the other monkeys would hand out a beating. There's nothing civil about the slave-like labor and extreme poverty that exists in all dictatorships worldwide.

If it were possible for a relative handful of super wealthy people to intentionally dumb-down the masses into little more than malleable imbeciles, would they? Just stop and think about how grown adults act when they get drunk. Drunk people are missing words, have lost any sense of shame, and are seeking food and sex. When the drunks are frequent enough, eventually the drinker becomes unable to perceive their now-diminished performance.

We've all been duped into self-administering this easy to obtain bio-logical weapons. Billionaires have sold us daily brain damage via TV programming in order for us to tolerate the otherwise intolerable world that they've engineered to control us. Two totally sober adults in public would rarely ever approach one another. However, throw consciousness killing alcohol into the equation (and as soon as normal brain activity has been lowered) our inhibitions brought on by societal control and belief systems quickly melt away. Our base primal urges take over and we then do what's on the lowest level of our needs chart. When we kill our consciousness, our top priorities are still on the lowest of levels. Adapt to escape a lifetime of rapey employers and shitty companions.

None of us can rely upon a miracle in a bottle without having it eventually backfire on us. Just like every other too-good-to-be true solution that we've come across, eventually there's a downside. Normally the good things that make us truly happy require some hard work, discipline, and some courage. When you stop drinking daily and unplug your cable box for an entire month, you might start to see that our leaders are just following orders from their higher-ups (not from the public).

In "Cinderella Man," working a tougher job for less money created a powerful left hook. 1%, you've toughened up Americans and made us less fearful. Good job. The few people that are pulling most of our strings know we're waking-up and are doing everything that they can to encourage constant public Soma use. Boosting your own consciousness through the few changes outlined in this book will give you more guts than when medicating daily. Lower paying jobs require more drinks, drugs, and TV programming to tolerate.

When you're completely awake and sober, please take a long look into the mirror at your own naked body. Is this the person that you've always wanted to become? We've all been intentionally conditioned into killing our own consciences to make us easier targets for billionaires to fleece. None of this is an accident. Not church, school, television programming or the beers that we drink after work while watching sports. This diet has made the public easily manageable by our loving elites. This way, we'll all do exactly what they want us to without ever figuring a way out of it.

There are constant beer and liquor commercials saying that alcohol will make things better. With enough repetition, it's hard for any TV-watching adult not to want to at least try it. For any of us with an even slightly stressful existence, (and God help us if we have an addictive personality) once we try the proposed stress reliever of alcohol or pills (sold by TV) we're hooked. It's not even a fair fight! If you show me infomercials, then I'll want to buy it.

How many people reading this have friends that are also addicted to coffee? They have to have their coffee every single day (all day). It's no longer a matter of choice. Most of the non-coffee drinkers (health nuts) in this world tend to be the people that naturally have high levels of self-motivation. In return, because they're more motivated than us, we call them nuts.

How many well-off people have we known that died in vain suffering from fear, anger, and resentments that dominated their thoughts and actions? How many of them also loved to have a few drinks? Perhaps a short viewing of the movie "There Will Be Blood" ought to prove my point. All of our leaders should have to piss in a cup daily just to prove that they're not drunks and drug addicts (just like the sheeple that blindly obey them).

This world has become overly dominated by sociopaths that also just so happen to be drunks and drug addicts. The "Wolf Of Wall Street" at least drove that point home. Wealthy sociopaths certainly don't care about the public and never will. More likely, the super wealthy are worried about their next drunk or high just like your trailer park neighbors are. Thank God for the vampire class on earth that the zombie public hasn't figured this out yet.

Steve Jobs may also qualify as a good example of a person that let health slip away while pursuing the black hole of material wealth. The movies about Mr. Jobs aren't exactly complimentary. The unquenchable thirst for more power and prestige is a tricky trap to escape when a corrupt world begins throwing more money at a human ego. My God have I gotten sucked in and thoroughly chewed up by the same cyclone of insanity that successfulness can do to an ego. Financial success can leave truck-sized blind spots all around you. I thought I was invincible, but Michelle proved otherwise. Would you like to outlive the ripe old age of 56? Mr. Jobs died still carrying resentment toward Bill Gates.

Being happy and healthy now is the best revenge against someone that harmed us in our past. Holding grudges against other people only hurts the grudge holder. Ironically, the biggest grudge that most of us have to forgive is with ourselves. This happens due to a lifetime of impossible to follow and conflicting rules. The wealthiest people don't follow these same impossible-to-follow rules that are being imposed on the rest of us.

Remember, it's over, gone, and done. Start enjoying what's in your life today. We can be better people today by the way that we treat other people and by the way that we treat ourselves. I've met several business owners during my own employment career that chased financial power to spiritual emptiness and early graves. The tremendous irony for a lot of wealthy Americans is that the very children that stand to inherit the financial fortunes (never enjoyed by their deceased parents) often resent the parent that died young pursuing more money. Many rich people are cursed with always planning for tomorrow while sacrificing today's happiness and kindness toward others. It's always about the pursuit of future benefits. If you try to live for the future, it's easy to miss the joy in today. Be kind today with your wallet and you'll actually feel good about yourself today.

We must embrace health and generosity. Otherwise we're inadvertently sucking the life out of the people around us. The term emotional vampire is worth looking into. Miserable people spend most of their time hoarding away a huge stash of money to be spent at a future date. What's the opposite of confidence?

If you suffer from anxiety and also drink often, smoke, or constantly pop pills to relieve said anxiety, then you're living in fear. Admitting this to ourselves is the first step to getting rid of a pitiful fear-based existence. One of the most stupid simple realizations that I made during my first year of sobriety was that coffee actually caused me to feel more anxiety than without it. I was shocked at what a huge effect one little cup of coffee had on me, but it did. I couldn't believe that something most people drink every day gave me such a definite feeling of anxiousness. When we're in fear, are we better or worse at solving problems? Then, later on in the day, what do we often reach for while on edge?

Simple activities are no longer easy for fearful people. We've been tricked by television to throw pills at our fear; pills, food, or alcohol. Does that sound about right? AA is a great place to quit drinking but just like rehab, at some point you need to rejoin the real world. Many AAers are guilty of turning a practical solution that can be done in a year into a lifelong cult that separates them from society. Tackle your addictions and then move on with life. Talking about your past for years on end keeps you trapped there. Get healthy and get on with life. We're not life-long victims. Drunk in a bar every day or spending years of your life in a multiple day per week cult of sobriety are both over-doing it.

I strongly advocate finding a happy medium and avoiding organized religions that demand all of your time and energy (and tell you that you're never done). Seven days a week drinking or talking about not drinking are both extreme. Coffee is nearly always on hand in the AA rooms because of a four-letter word (in my book) called tradition. Incredibly with extreme consistency, when I introduced coffee into my own system, I then experienced fear. Would billionaires want the working class to be physically addicted to fear-inducing substances? Cigarettes and alcohol aren't the go-to staples of relief for tens of millions of working-poor Americans by accident. Greedy business owners prefer having anxious employees.

If there's one thing that the absolute poorest people in America (homeless people) share in common, it's coffee, cigarettes, and alcohol. Does that sound about right? Are they mentally well? Getting millions of people hooked on anxiety-causing products that then get treated with daily sedation (all for profit) is brilliant. Make even more money while keeping the moronic slave class as fearful and later sedated as possible. Be a good zombie and keep following the slow zombie diet.

We're the only creatures on earth that must chemically knock ourselves out at night after ingesting fear-inducing stimulants all day (that are sold to us by our trustworthy overlords). We sure are smart. If you're a really classy addict then you pop Dr. approved pill-bottle not-give-a-crap (Ambien) every single night before bed. If you T-chart real people in your own life, then you'll likely find that the heaviest people with failing health share coffee, pills, and daily alcohol in common. Oh yes, and diet soda. If there's one thing that seems to wreck human bodies faster than anything, it's diet soda (with brain numbing aspartame).

Did you know that aspartame (found in diet soda) breaks down into wood alcohol in the human body once it warms above 85 degrees? Look this up. We're not all permanently dumber. The effects of the zombie diet are very much reversible. We're only temporarily weakened by these weapons of mass sedation that can quickly be flushed from our systems. The miraculous reversal from poor health and daily suffering to feeling and looking good can happen in months, not years.

Chapter 6 – Traditions Shared With Walmart Zombies

Traditions exist only until the majority decides that there's a better way of doing things. Are some Americans ready to admit that the way we've been doing things isn't working out so well for us? Many of us have nothing left to lose. Even our pride can be set aside in the face of personal disaster. Even gay pride may be a bit under thought out. You're proud to have the right to be married? Now you can get contractually stuck in a relationship where the other person stops trying as hard to keep you with them. If you do decide to leave a partner that has become totally unfair, you'll lose half of your stuff if not everything. Divorce attorneys (pampered rich kids) can't wait to get their hands on divorced gay people's hard-earned life savings.

We do all agree that a chunk of both parties' life savings gets consumed by legal fees in every divorce. I honestly don't care who marries who and am all for equal rights. Good luck enjoying millions of relationships where the more selfish partner is about to start acting a lot more selfish. I'm willing to bet that lawyers supply substantial funding for gay marriage legislation in every state. It's like a council of vampires trying to pass legislation that'll start construction of new blood banks in every town across America. Greedy rich kids need some way to keep that half million dollar house and the Mercedes in the driveway. There's a huge market share to be tapped into. Gay people ought not be prevented from all of the logic and reason that entering into a legal marriage has delivered to straight people. About half of the married men that I see look like they want to be shot in the head. Sign me up.

The only thing keeping many disgruntled people married is the intense fear of breaking the contract and loosing half of their stuff; that, and alcoholism. To all future gay people that are marrying for money: Alcohol and anti-depressants are the best way to financially drain your next victim while keeping them too unaware to see the true nature of the relationship. Parasitic spouses that are only in relationships for the money heavily depend on the regular sedation of their partners.

The absolute best way to learn from other people is to look at an entire institution that has failed more than half of its participants (resulting in intense pain and financial ruin) and then, copy those people. Rather than trying a slightly different approach, we just copy all of our friends, family, and co-workers that have crashed and burned right in front of our eyes. We do the exact same activity that they did and expect different results.

How many of us know wonderful and thoughtful people that have suffered great destruction from a bad divorce? People have proven over and over again that they can behave well enough for just long enough to get married. Only on a planet of talking monkeys would such an obviously flawed contract continue to exist without being modified. If your marriage is out of love, then you don't need a piece of paper to enforce rules. The belief that legal marriages will provide you a better behaving life-long romantic partner is ridiculous. This is just as insane as believing that politicians who swear an oath will better serve the people.

The least honest people in our current society seem to be the most eager to get into long-term contracts promising decent people future services. Our wives, husbands, and politicians don't deserve contractually obligated terms lasting years, let alone months or even days. These contracts only set up the more honest partner for a lengthier period of abuse. Look out if your dependant partner sends you to the doctor to start taking anti-depressants or brings you home alcohol during the week and encourages you to constantly be drunk. If so, you're likely being used for your financial resources like a drunken cow being kept in a stall for milking. Moooooooohh!

Marriage has always seemed like a horrifically thought-out line of reasoning to me. Perhaps that's why a mirage and marriage are so closely related to one another in spelling. It's a fantastic illusion that looks very promising from a distance, but once you get there you get less sex and less effort in all other areas from the more selfish partner.

I'm pro love, pro loyalty, and pro affection with one monogamous partner for as long as the relationship is loving and honest for both partners. Kids benefit greatly from having two loving parents with different strengths while growing up. Getting married is an honorable action that is ideal for raising families. All we need to do is completely remove the chance for financial gain from lawyers and dishonest spouses. Take a crooked legal system out of the equation and leave in the love and commitment.

With the infinite number of examples where a seemingly good partner turns terrible after the contract has been signed, why doesn't the standard marriage contract eliminate any chance for financial gain? There sure would be a lot less wrinkly old men with hot young wives. Plus, those delusional old men (many of which are drunks) would stop getting secretly cheated on by their gold digging wives.

Old men with strikingly beautiful wives that are clearly there for the money must stop kidding themselves that a money worshipping woman wouldn't also be sleeping with younger studs on the side. True loyalty cannot be purchased. People without consciences don't want just anything, they want everything. When they get that, it still won't be enough. God help these tortured souls that make up a minority of humanity. Drunken husbands and wives may not see this happening, but sober ones do. They cease to remain long-term victims of sociopaths that are only using them for their energy. The health of the partner that's being vamped off of nearly always declines.

We all know lots of people with miserable husbands and wives that they stay with out of fear. Fear is what keeps them trapped in parasitic relationships. Often, the egos of fearful people will do stupendous gymnastics and convince them that they are brave for spending a lifetime getting crapped on. God knows the truth.

These are the types of deals that we allow ourselves to become contractually obligated to (often for a set number of years). What an insane premise this is in a country full of not-so-bright people. The moment that there's no longer a line of unintelligent

71

customers willing to hand over their money for an unfair deal, that particular business will cease to exist.

What a horrible world it would be if sociopathic people everywhere suddenly became obvious to the public and couldn't catch their food. Congressional terms should be limited to a month-by-month basis with the public's right to cancel at anytime. It's funny how single people that are dating for months or even years at a time remain youthful. The moment that contract is signed both husbands and wives pack on the pounds and adopt the scooter chair diet.

After no less than hundreds of examples of seeing the exact same types of contracts re-negotiated in the real world, we just keep signing up for them. Drunkeness and television have a lot to do with buying lies that nearly always fail to deliver on what was originally promised to us. These long term contracts with flawed humans (that aren't spiritually awake) rob us of our health and energy.

Inviting a spiritually asleep person into your own life is like inviting a vampire to come sleep on your couch for a few years. Not putting two and two together while your health slowly fails (and you wake up feeling like crap every morning) is pretty dumb. Emotional vampires do exist. To escape detection, they depend heavily on partners that have drinking and pill habits. If you're clearly an alcoholic that drinks daily, (and your poorer partner doesn't) who do you think has the upper hand in manipulating the other?

Emotional vampires are simply parasitic people that seem to feed off of others money and anger. They're always creating situations that upset their partners to obtain that next meal of anger. Drunks and drug addicts make the easiest long-term victims for emotional vampires to spend years feeding off of. If you're the person with the larger income and a larger drinking habit, then your partner who drinks less is more easily able to manipulate you.

Who wants to admit that they're part of a largely flawed institution that a healthier person refuses to participate in. For most American adults, heading into marriage is a lot like heading into the

72

Presidency. Almost immediately your hair begins to turn grey, you get serious wrinkles and look ten years older after four.

Relying on a legal system owned and operated by the rich people's network is a joke. Rich people will only begin to fear the working class, if just a handful of the super wealthy were held accountable. A few years in country club prison while the rest of us spend a lifetime in poverty isn't cutting it. Maybe that was the point of making the movie, "The Wolf of Wall Street." Even Bernie Madoff (appropriate name) gets food, shelter, and likely lives more comfortably than the working poor of America. It's not called the criminal justice system by mistake.

If 150,000 years of human evolution has taught us anything, it's that other humans that we enter into legal contracts with for a set number of years tend to treat us the best. That is, if we like being treated like crap. If you hire a prostitute for a 4 year contract, is that prostitute going to line up as many side customers as possible? What's the difference between that logic and our current political system? Do rings around married people's fingers stop them from violating the contract if they so happen to come across a better deal? We all know that our politicians have been offered millions of dollars to do whatever billionaires and corporations tell them to. Stop giving these people so much credit.

We should trust our politicians about as much as we trust our strippers, for a few minutes at a time while they're physically on our laps. Sure enough, that person that charmed you and made a soul connection with you thirty minutes earlier will be on the highest bidder's lap before you can drive home. Our politicians are more like money robot prostitutes than defenders of the Constitution. Corporations have driven up the price of these whores so drastically that the public can't afford five minutes. We know this is true. The will to actually do something about this is being uploaded right now.

When are we finally going to leave the strip club and seek out other people that aren't drug addicts that had loveless relationships with their fathers? Prime example: George W. Bush. The crazy thing is, several of our recent U.S. Presidents lacked good relationships with their fathers and likely have some additional skeletons in their closets. Bill Clinton: Daddy issues. George W. Bush: Daddy issues. Barack Obama: Daddy issues.

How many of us have tried to have healthy and loving relationships with known addicts suffering from daddy issues? The chances of receiving a fair deal when bargaining with these types of people is somewhere between not going to happen, and what the hell were you thinking? People with these traumatic issues shouldn't be groomed to be the future leaders of the free world, but they are.

Horrifically, that's exactly why the true powers that be have selected them to be the front men of America. Some people are predisposed to being compromised. Those personality types are then selected by king-makers that know they'll be able to steer the leader in the desired direction. The CIA is known to have developed a trauma-based mind control program called MK Ultra decades ago.

Have you ever dated somebody that had a traumatic childhood? Was the first six months when the other person put forth the most effort to treat you the best or not? What happens to the more selfish partners actions the second that a couple decides to move in together or gets married? Some very scarred and damaged people simply aren't satisfied unless they feel as if they're getting away with something. It's sad, but some people that were damaged as children will continue on exerting revenge against the rest of the world for the remainder of their lives. If we're trying to pick out conscientious leaders for the free world, then a loving and nurturing childhood would certainly help out our chances. In dictatorships, you'll often find that their dear leader's childhood was anything but loving and nurturing.

Scarred and self-centered people are most definitely reliant upon the steady energy supply that the traditions of marriage and political office supply to them. I'm tired of being the energy supply for parasitic people that are emotionally damaged and totally abusive toward the rest of us. They have no right to feed off of me and I'm showing all of their victims how the scammers operate. Do you want to continue being somebody else's drunken meal ticket until they've slowly bled you dry?

The only thing that our politicians sell us, are future promises that never come true. Just like the "Wolf of Wall Street" our politicians continue to live like drunken kings (while we don't). We know this is true. Only a country of hopeless drunks and pill heads would fail to do anything about it. We're their marks and they have no conscience left to care, and no one is coming to save us. We must unplug our own TV set and go find other people that escaped from the same problems that we currently have.

Being married and raising a family is a wonderful tradition, but perhaps the lawyers and contracts that have only empowered the more vampiristic types of people in our society need to be heavily rethought and re-written. The vampires have been writing the rules of our society for the last 5000 years. I vote that people with consciences re-write the rules that govern our lives in a way that lets all of the vampires starve out.

Another common part of our lives that relates to being easy prey is our overdependence on coffee. For the first 32 years of my life, I remained a non-coffee drinker. After only a few days of drinking a single cup of coffee per day did I begin to experience anxiety and nervousness that hadn't existed in the 32 years prior. People that have known me for a lifetime know that I'm not a fearful person.

Despite me figuring out that the coffee was what made me feel new anxiety, I continued drinking it for another week. I was hooked, that quick; as are millions of stressed-out people reading this (that are also part of America's rapidly growing victim class). If nearly everyone in the 50 million strong food stamp army drinks coffee every day, than I'm not.

I now live in a country that's filled with fearful people. The only time these same people feel confident is when they've popped their prescription anti-anxiety pills (legal drugs), or have deluded their self image with alcohol. I'm sick and tired of catering to the delusional egos of fearful Americans that badly need rehab and a hug. Somebody needs to be honest with these people so that they can begin to get help. Why are healthy people allowing a bunch of physically and mentally ill people to become the new American norm? There are now sitcoms featuring bloated Americans (norms).

Just because the average working class Joe hasn't put 2 and 2 together doesn't mean that something isn't easily solved. How many farm animals spend a lifetime in one small field that's guarded by a few small electrical wires and a paper-thin fence? What's keeping those animals in that field? I would argue that fear, stupidity, and apathy are the answers. That, and guaranteed meals that are provided by their owners with zero effort required. Do many of those animals die of natural causes or get slaughtered for food?

Dressing things up with prettier words doesn't change who and what we've become. Some of my own traits that had to be abandoned (in order to survive) were very much relatable to the negative character traits featured in both Steve Jobs movies. We're all flawed and are constantly making mistakes while living this human experience. The point is, we're supposed to be learning and not intentionally hurting other people all day long to benefit ourselves. Treat others how you'd like to be treated; it's that simple.

After linking coffee consumption to my own past anxiety, I decided to post this epiphany on my Facebook page. The non-brand specific post connecting coffee to anxiety (daily fear) was deleted by Facebook immediately. The posting simply stated that many people are addicted to coffee that likely makes them anxious during the day. They then drink alcohol or take prescription pills at night (which they're also addicted to) to relieve their anxiety. Not profound, but it was deleted.

David Icke beautifully explains how problem, reaction, solution is used by the few to control the many. Our ego is the part of our psyche that will lie to us and tell us that we're in control when we're not. Nobody wants to admit that they've become addicted to anything. We don't want to feel powerless over our own behaviors. Our dogs are powerless over lots of behaviors too aren't they?

We love to think that we're so far separated from lower-level animals, but we're really just the best dressed apes in the partially-paved jungle. Food, sex, shelter, and the money to get it all is where most talking apes are at right now. The ability to create, repair complex machines, or simply empathize with similar people is beyond public reach. All of this can change, and is.

Everything is now watched and under surveillance, all in the name of safety (fear). This all took place after our leaders used television to scare the dignity out of us on 911. Even if they didn't plan or allow the attacks to happen, they certainly repeated the image of the planes hitting the buildings and the buildings imploding, no less than hundreds of times. The repetition was part of the training process. It was like watching a loved one get run down by a car and being forced to re-watch the accident hundreds of times. It was mass mind control and it worked perfectly.

We were all suspects in the interrogation room on some cop show being forced to watch a traumatic video over and over again. Eventually we can't handle the image anymore, and will do anything that the person playing the video asks of us. Did we go along with a huge increase in airport security, internet spying, and phone tapping? It was all in the name of not showing us that horrible video anymore.

Eventually, all that our beloved politicians had to do was simply mention the word 911, and we all jump before they play the awful video again. We all got psychologically scarred that day. We were all fearful enough and therefore dumb enough to go along with the con. This is how mass mind control works. Freak somebody out really bad with a traumatic event, and then take control of the situation while the person's brain is still in panic mode.

We all know that the logic in our heads gets shut-off during traumatic events. We then go into fight or flight mode and end up thinking more like primates than people. As a country, we've acted like a bunch of children that took a severe beating from our parent with a belt. Every time that our politicians want to get us back into a state of fear, they only have to show us the belt and say the magic word, 911. Trauma based mind control was used on all of us. That damage is being repaired right now.

Our heads were hacked by a few sociopathic individuals that have lied their way into positions of power. All of their malicious programs are being deleted right now. We're not a fear-based Republic filled with neutered males (no matter how hard the media's been inflating the feminine men's appeal). Women in the real world still go after high testosterone males. There's been a war on natural male characteristics in America while the economy has steadily declined. It's ok for both divine masculine and feminine traits to exist.

Do you want to continue being manipulated by wealthy sociopaths in suits on TV? I don't. If a bully takes his belt off to scare a room full of kids, then I'm going after him. We used to have movies that showed these kind of images like "Indiana Jones and the Temple of Doom" where Harrison Ford takes on the over-sized man whipping children down in the mines. Only after the slaves see someone else stand-up to the slave master do they begin to overrun the badly outnumbered guards. Our politicians deserve the same treatment after their shameless abuse of the word 911 on our TV sets. All of it was a program, and that program is being dismantled right now.

There's video evidence of this claim. We don't attack the politicians that have betrayed us; we ignore them and leave them with empty venues. They can give their deceptive speeches in empty rooms that nobody is paying attention to anymore. If you want the politicians to stop whipping you with words, then turn off your TV. It's like taking the whip out of the whip master's hand. I'm no longer afraid of the greedy old men that are no longer holding a mental whip over me. I'm not even paying attention to them. Refuse to watch TV and their whip is gone. It's this easy.

Of all the 18-55 year-olds making up the U.S. workforce, how many of us use alcohol or mood enhancing pills just to cope with life? We all know that this is true, but we're pretending that half of the population isn't all drugged up and half drunk all of the time. How often do average Americans get buzzed? If I'm trying to pick the losing horses in the human race, then I'm betting on the ones that can't stop from getting drunk every day or popping tons of pills. This too can change right now. Newfound hope files are being installed for those who need them.

Are you just another one of the dejected voters that dare not challenge the whip masters of our society? If you truly refuse to watch TV and stop drinking liquid anxiety (coffee) every day, then you'll soon have the guts to look over at the man that once held the whip and see that it's gone. The terror in a bully's eyes when you're coming at them is something that a loving God would approve of. No loving God would want us to live lifetimes of fear while bowing down to evil men. Good parents that raise respectable people are proud when they see their little kid stand up to a big bully. Bullies often pick on the weak and the unhealthy. A large group of diminished selves is the only way our corrupted leaders have stolen so much so fast without pushback.

The average physical health of Americans has gotten significantly worse in the last 30 years. If you're not sure about this statement, just watch any movie from the 1970's like "Caddie Shack" and observe how skinny all of the extras are. That's what most of us used to look like. If we're being honest, average has gotten a whole lot fatter. Whatever activities are the most common of the dumbest, fattest and most fearful people need to be abandoned. When we do so, we'll find new strength and speed. Most people that are now surrounded by addicts fail to call them out on their bullshit.

Just let someone else deal with it; that has become the new national anthem. My suggested brand of consciousness is totally different from the coffee drinking, smoking old men of AA (who all get government checks). The brand of sobriety from 1940 is no longer effective during the internet age. All or nothing can't be expected to be followed forever, that's also going to extremes. What I'm proposing is quitting for long enough to regain self-control and to address personal problems that daily drunkenness and prescription pills have failed to address. Once you've regained self-control, try to find a happy medium that allows you to rejoin society without claiming to be damaged for life.

My personal experience with the AA program is that it did help me stop drinking. However, the rooms are littered with long-term members claiming years of sobriety that haven't addressed their other issues. I don't propose staying there forever. Once you've regained health and balance, wean yourself off of the rehab group. Otherwise, it can become just as isolating as Scientology or any other 7 day per week cult. In general, our society avoids 7 day per week fanatics. Find balance and long-term moderation. Let old AA-Nazis throw a fit when you regain your personal health and re-join society. One dirty secret that I discovered prior to leaving the AA rooms behind me was that many of the long-term old timers in the program were also taking prescription anti-depressants.

AA has something like a 3-5% lifetime success rate meaning that roughly 95% of society eventually decides to walk away (like I did, because their promises weren't coming true). So far as I understand, about 20% of ex-problem drinkers remain non-problem drinkers in the absence of AA after initially quitting. Only 3% of AA people maintain continual sobriety until they die. The point is, a lot of ex-drinkers use AA to quit, and then leave the rooms after gaining some long-term sobriety.

My warning is that our modern day court system has been mandatorily funneling sociopaths into the AA program for a few decades. A person (with no criminal record) that starts hanging around in rooms with convicted felons and repeat offenders several nights per week shouldn't be surprised when things other than their drinking fail to get better. "Southpark" did an AA episode, and I can hardly argue with it. If the writers weren't at all concerned about some possible risks of the program, then they wouldn't have taken the time to make an episode about it. Many Americans have attempted to play the victim-for-life card.

Unplug the TV, quit drinking coffee, and stop knocking yourself out each night. That's the zombie diet; that, and our self-administered fluoride doses each day that we've been trained to administer since childhood. Your fluoride toothpaste does decrease your problem solving abilities, because fluoride is a known neurotoxin. Harvard studies have shown that fluoride ingestion actually lowers IQ over the course of time.

The corporations selling us this diet don't care if they're perpetuating bad relationships and horrible jobs. They don't care about your true quality of life. They want the most work for as little money as possible (and they're getting it). You're simply a target, and they're aiming straight for your brain. The billionaires decide the policies of the FDA. Perhaps the FDA has rigged the system to get the most work from the American sheeple as possible. Would rich peoples' consciences allow such a thing?

Between overuse of TV, fluoride, aspartame, coffee, alcohol, and weed, our workforce has never been so apathetic. We've become pushovers accepting degrading treatment for $10 per hour all across America (while food prices have doubled). What part of prescription drugs prevents us from realizing that we've become dependent upon mind altering drugs? Is this what the previous 4900 years of civilized human beings were doing? We've been conned on a massive scale by the very people claiming to provide us with solutions.

Perhaps pills and drinks that numb us to the worst situations in life may also be numbing us to the greatest gifts that this lifetime can offer. We can't have it both ways. These easy fixes have also been robbing us of our God-given perceptive abilities. If the majority of people are bloated and limping through the streets, then perhaps we should start avoiding the doctors that those same people go to.

What do you think prescription anti-depressants are? Just because a Dr. (drug distribution expert) has had expensive schooling, doesn't mean that he or she won't push aside morals in the name of money. The pills aren't addressing our true problems. Many doctors, lawyers, and politicians are functioning alcoholics and prescription drug-addicts at this very moment. If you were once really really smart and now find yourself immersed in a society full of idiots, then drinking frequently in order to blend in makes perfect sense. TV only shows them at their best.

Abandon well-dressed criminals that deal only in empty promises (that never deliver). They've stayed wealthy while we've all become poorer. The game has been rigged. Walk off of their chess board and let them panic. The public makes or breaks businesses. Billion dollar empires can fall overnight. The general public holds the true power.

Are there people in your own life that are definitely alcoholics, yet have no trouble keeping their job? We just trust the alcoholic doctors, lawyers and politicians because they happen to be dressed up in expensive suits while they're giving us advice (selling us out). They also had rich parents to afford sufficient legal defenses against life-wrecking events in poor peoples' lives like DUIs. For how long are we going to keep trusting con artist children that only stayed out of legal trouble via upper-class pardons? Once you've been shown how a particular scam works, you then become one less person that falls for it. We're not being ruled over by moral leaders.

Am I at all concerned about being knocked-off by corrupt men because I'm shining light on their primary bio-logical (affecting our logic) weapons? No. We have no freedom at all if we're too afraid to speak freely. I believe in life after death and can't continue watching people get abused without speaking up. I've watched multiple business owners driving high-dollar cars effortlessly shove an endless line of suitable victims into the meat grinder of unlivable wages called their business. Over and over again throughout the creation of this book I've witnessed owners taking far more energy than they give. We can change this by no longer serving evil people. It all starts with us.

Chapter 7 – The Zombie Apocalypse Already Happened

Our enemies prefer that we remain slightly sedated, hopeless, and disorganized as a group. This way we're much easier to control. Slow moving drunken zombies are the zombies that I want to be outrunning if I'm taxing the dumb bastards without representing them. Definitely not, fast smart zombies. Have you been in a Walmart lately? If you were a billionaire genius walking down the aisles of Walmarts across America right this minute, what do you see everywhere?

The zombie apocalypse (change) has already happened. In the eyes of a genius, you're likely one of them. This is the part where an accurate mirror is being placed in front of your face (and many of you let out a long slow groaning noise). It's ok, you're experiencing a shift in consciousness.

Wouldn't you prefer running your brain and heart on full power again? Has your memory gotten better or worse since you were a teenager? It only became painfully obvious to me just how blind I had once been after completely removing alcohol, fluoride, and TV from my daily routine for several months. The increased perception, peace, and love felt toward humanity are well worth a few weeks of total weirdness. You'll begin to look and feel better within weeks. Remember, you're reading words I've written. You're not seeing the actual positive nature of my face to face interactions with positive people in the real world. This book has spread to other people one person at a time, starting with strangers that are interested in something that I have (that's unusual).

Walking proof of positive results is how you spread an idea to your neighbors. Since 2008 the U.S. economy has crashed and the American zombies have done nothing to make things better (because they're generally zonked-out). Only addicts stay in abusive situations and do absolutely nothing to get out of them. We can all make things better by simply trying.

Clearly our leaders on TV didn't stop millions of Americans from losing good jobs, houses, and often families that got blown to bits by the financial storm of 2008. We've taken a severe beating as a country and need to stop whining about our sad plight to our drunken friends that can't help us to get out of this. If you copy the coping strategies of down-and-out people from the poor parts of town, then that's where you'll stay. If this economy has wrecked you too, then find someone else that also got wrecked but has put themselves back together again with improvements. If you lay down with whooped dogs, you get fleas.

We must fight for each other because the leaders on TV aren't fighting for us. When are we going to stop being conned by the guy wearing the most expensive suit on TV? The veil is being lifted. It all just might be a ride, but if your ride's feeling like a lengthy nightmare, then change it already. Each one of us has the power to change our own ride.

Our group's consciousness has been purposely lowered to make us more obedient marks. Would rich men sabotage the brains of the public by intentionally selling us a low-consciousness diet? It's time to start waking up the zombies. Our entire country seems to have been sucked into the same socially acceptable cult, the church of the holy bottles. It's wrecked our bodies and made us poor.

The church of the holy bottles makes its priests and ushers wealthy while the rest of the congregation slips further into poverty. As long as it's an orange bottle with a Doctor's name on the side, then it's a guilt-free escape from reality that must be done daily in order to take your beatings. The completely defeated low-wage workers of Cleveland, Ohio were such a shining example of this. Like in most ghettos, weed was also everywhere where the most downtrodden workers remained stuck for life.

Then there's the equally ridiculous daily worship of the other type of bottle for those classy intellectuals that simply like the taste of wine, (daily) and no less than a bottle at a time. Never has the human ego masked an excuse for a daily drunk better than a semi-wealthy wine drinker. These are perhaps the proudest and most delusional of all of the walking dead in America. Wine drinking alcoholics are still alcoholics.

After living with and growing to love an entire family of rednecks in Georgia I've gotta say, at least beer-drinking rednecks are halfway honest with themselves when accepting that they're alcoholics. They at least admit that they need their daily buzz just to function. College educated business professionals have woven a web of self-deception that seems fortified by the pride that goes along with an expensive college degree. Both blue collar and white collar people are equally vulnerable to getting caught by the holy bottle.

The church of the holy bottle destroys self-respect, ruins good relationships, and perpetuates bad ones. Nothing great comes from the path of least resistance. It's about time to start resisting the daily habits that our ownership-class would love to see continue. They don't care about us and prefer that we keep seeking alcohol and pills for escape, because the escape never works. Weed doesn't work either.

If only the Russian people had Stalin-phones and food cards people would see the parallels. If I have to be a zombie, (and there are hundreds of millions of us in the United States) then I choose to be a fast smart zombie. When I bite, people get smarter and healthier. They begin to take gutsier actions and stop acting like subservient dogs. This is truly the zombie disease that billionaires are the most terrified of, the spread of consciousness from one freed mind to another. All of this time, the greatest fear of wealthy men around the world has been the spread of knowledge.

There are a few movies that are excellent analogies for why it's time to raise the consciousness of the suffering public. They are: Rise Of The Planet Of The Apes, Rise Of The Lycans, Day Breakers, and Warm Bodies. All four movies beautifully illustrate the super wealthy keeping the masses under their constant control. Only while we remain slightly dumber and constantly sedated can the ruling elites maintain their edge.

Each movie portrays a weaker slave class that finally gets woken up and takes back power from corrupt leaders. Remember, a single person can't physically control millions of people that are equally as intelligent as themselves. The greedy few that own our leaders must keep the masses in a zombie-like state for the con-game to continue.

A horrible parent that wants a small child to stay quiet and occupied could simply hand them an I-pad and a spill-proof cup of apple juice spiked with Jim Beam. This is pretty well what smart phones, flat screen TVs, and the religion of pro sports has done to former grown adults in America. Most adults now perform their jobs and then are immediately sedated and entertained into a near-retarded state of consciousness each and every day.

Once the average American can see lies, they become a Lycan, as in the movie, "Rise of the Lycans." Don't vampires wear amulets around their necks for protection? Somehow the dumbest zombies amongst us seem to be falling for a similar trick. Sociopathic people will tattoo crosses on themselves or wear them around their necks. Incredibly, it works as an invisibility cloak for them to rip off zombies without startling the poor dumb bastards. Nazis wore crosses too while slaughtering their way across Europe. A cross around a person's neck means nothing about their moral character.

Jesus revealed to people that God is within all of us. Sociopathic politicians and priests wearing ceremonial suits that are always requiring weekly offerings (taxes) for protection are frauds. If you've read the entire new testament, that's what it's all about. Jesus exposed the sham of the government and its citizen mind-control systems during his own time. The Roman authorities crucified him because his words inspired the peasant class to seek true spirituality from within. Jesus empowered people.

As a group, we're already far more powerful than all politicians and billionaires combined. We simply have to realize it and start working together to unveil the current control system that's been keeping us poor. Wars around the world have only been perpetuated by this same vampire class of kings, priests and politicians. It actually takes a whole lot of provocation and cheap tricks to get the citizenry into conflicts. You now have the choice to remove your own mind-controlling collar and will have the knowledge of how to do it. All of the shadiest men and women on earth are about to start needing some anxiety medication.

Chapter 8 – Televised Sedatives For Zombies

I reference movies because our population has been massively conditioned to spend hours upon hours in front of a screen that, as David Icke says, "Tells us a vision." Is the TV telling you your own vision or somebody else's? Our brains make powerful connections based on what we see and hear from these screens. Have you ever heard of a type of screen that's able to hide something (dangerous) that's coming?

The ruling elites that vainly attempt to quench their unquenchable thirst for money and power have successfully used our TV's against us as a smoke screen to hide their true intentions. This is a tough pill for the human ego to swallow. Accepting that we've been tricked into mentally weakening ourselves for an entire lifetime (to be their tax base) sounds horrible, but that doesn't mean that it's not true. Our energy (that's been siphoned off in the form of taxes) has been used not to protect us, but to build up a massive surveillance system with one true purpose; to protect the parasitic politicians and bankers from the public that they feed off of.

Wizards use a staff made of holy wood to cast spells on ignorant people. Aren't there staffs in Hollywood that cast spells on the public now? Surely you know some grown adults that are still terrified of swimming in the ocean because of a movie called "Jaws" from forty years ago, right? Logic can be easily destroyed and abandoned by the magic of Hollywood. Since the widespread distribution of television sets and movie theatres, controlling the general public in places like Nazi Germany, Communist Russia and right here in America has been child's play. If the controllers begin to lose their grip on power, they simply produce a new fear-based event (like 911).

Showing a few rich and greedy men already lacking morals or a conscience that kind of power was too good to pass up. They haven't. If you were a bad guy that had the resources to produce a movie or television show that would get millions of people to behave exactly how you wanted them to, could you pass up that opportunity? How many Starbucks were open for business in the United States before the TV show "Friends" came out? A stranger did propose to me that instead, the U.S. coffee shop explosion was a bunch of aging baby-boomers that were settling down and switching from cocaine to coffee. I personally think that people mimic their TV sets.

Go back to the year that "Friends" first showed really good looking and funny people hanging out at a coffee shop. How many Starbucks were open nationwide back then? Fast forward to the year of the final episode of "Friends" and see how many Starbucks were in operation. At the same time, our country experienced an explosion in prescription anti-anxiety medication. The market share for pills that relieve anxiety exploded simultaneously. Suddenly, half of the U.S. population is now diseased for life and can't live without their medication (active drug habit). Television drives trends. More importantly, it drives behavior. How many American women suddenly had "Rachel" haircuts?

We might as well be monkeys watching a video and then copying the behaviors that we see. Please keep taking your obedience medication. Don't do activities like working out, going for walks, or helping other people; all of which naturally release chemicals in your brain that make you feel happier. Either half of our country has actually gone crazy, or the vast majority of those people not born with mental illness are now totally full of shit.

Were more than half of the Nazi German people mentally well? How about the North Korean people that are being completely dominated for their lifetimes? Millions of Russians and Chinese people starved to death while systems of "equality" were implemented in their countries. Were they well? Is the general public well? Perhaps not copying their TV programming, coffee, weed, and prescribed anti-depressant regimens is worth straying away from. There are plenty of failing groups of people with stupid daily routines scattered across the world. People get conquered, and often by stealth.

Do you really think that a just and loving God or a race of advanced beings would respect any of this? People get lied to on a massive scale, and sociopathic control freaks carry out science experiments with the public (as if we're lab rats). They believe that we're all so hopelessly stupid and inferior to them that we should have no say about what the next experiment will be. Many super-predators survived World War II. Do you suspect these were obvious predators, or stealthy assholes? Guess who got pardoned in invited into the US propaganda machine after world war II?

One on one confrontations may support meathead alpha males, but massive populations have been decimated by social control programs created by omega males. Words alone contain incredible power. Saying the right thing at the right time can be enough to save a person's life. A bombardment of information in the right combination can transform defeated citizens into empowered people. Words alone can set people free. This is why all dictatorships must eventually eliminate free speech.

Most of us do have consciences and don't want that much power in life. Nor do we want to control and manipulate the whole group as we see fit. Life has taught us that power corrupts. As a result, most of us decent people have completely avoided politics. We've seen too many other people that started out with good intentions but later got corrupted. Politics doesn't sound like an appealing career to get into (unless you want power and enjoy swimming in snakes).

When we get power, it tends to go right to our heads. Perhaps that was the point of the "Lord of The Rings" books and movies. One of the greatest illusions ever pulled off by the elite (via our TV sets) is the illusion of choice in a two party system. Both parties are paid-for and owned by the same small group of super wealthy elites that share a common interest, to stay in power. Picture a presidential debate on television as nothing more than a giant puppeteer under the stage playing his right hand puppet against his left.

We're like a whole country of retarded children attempting to ride a dead horse. It's time to get a new vehicle or start riding the bus. Will I be sitting on a urine-smelling bus with a bunch of half-dead people while millionaires fly past us all in their brand new

Mercedes? No. Empowering working-class Americans will drive the vampire class of America crazy. Our Congressmen should also be forced to only consume the exact same food being distributed to public schools nationwide per Michelle Obama's lunch program.

All political leaders that are currently in favor of forced inoculations should also be inoculated with multiple flu shots and vaccines that contain mercury within their preservatives. To this day, flu shots nationwide and vaccines contain both aluminum and mercury. However, Sarah Palin is portrayed as a moron on TV and also is opposed to forced vaccinations. Therefore, all Americans not wanting brain damage brought about by injecting known neurotoxins into their bodies are now deemed dumb rednecks by politically correct people (that believe their news anchors with a religious fervor).

All anti-vaccine people must be dancing around inside of churches while holding snakes and bobbing around on the floor together. Zero intellectuals must have ever investigated claims about vaccines and found that serious risks do exist. Massive damages have been paid-out by pharmaceutical companies relating to vaccines, but the risks must be zero as stated by busty blondes and brunettes on TV. My favorite beer is also sold by busty blondes and brunettes.

All of those anti-vaccine kooks must not believe in science or logic. They're all ignorant, and there's no such thing as a scientist in any country that has a tyrannical system of control. I'm sure that scientists that are desperate to provide their families food and shelter would never fudge the numbers in order to remain employed in a corrupt country.

The world has changed in many ways and we must adapt using logic, common sense, and principles of freedom. Old belief systems must be modified due to the present challenges that face us. Individual rights are worth saving along with the group that we belong to. A handful of massive sociopaths will go down swinging, and that's just fine with me.

Corporations and world bankers own our elected officials. Our own TV tells us that Congress has a 10% approval rating. For

Congress to still be employed by us makes no sense. Our protections from government have failed us and we're failing ourselves. The "will of the people" is no longer being served. This is the truth and we know it. Our ancestors have booted greedy sociopaths out of power before and so will we. Resistance to tyranny is ingrained in our DNA.

When the zombified public starts raising their consciousness back up again, the dingy strip club lighting gets turned back on bright. Then our politicians will begin to start looking like the skanky prostitutes that they really are. What do you think these guys look like when you take them out of their thousand dollar suits? Put them in a pair of shorts and a white tee-shirt (with no TV makeup on) and they start to look like Walmart people to me. Screw their infinite supply of future promises that never come true. We are better than this and can find better people to help run things. In fact, 99% of us that actually do run factories, manage business, and do all of the actual labor are already running things. Local governance does work as opposed to global governance that psychopath world elites are pushing for.

The super wealthy that do understand how to manipulate us don't view the public as equally valuable people. Instead, they see targets. What part of your body do you think they're aiming for? Are you getting the zombie metaphor yet? They don't use guns to shoot for the head. They use TV, alcohol, drugs, and anything that renders us all brain dead. The few want the many to stay as unaware as possible (of their scams) for the rest of our lives. That way, we'll stay poor and hopeless and they get to dominate the rest of us for our lifetime.

The way that the public can terrify as many billionaires as much as possible is by unplugging ourselves from our TV programming. Do you like the idea of millions of Americans behaving in a way that drives terror into the hearts of billionaires? In fact, the less that we fear the establishment, the more terror they'll begin broadcasting on TV. If we've stopped watching (criminal) network TV, then we'll stop fearing fabricated stories designed to continue controlling us.

What if it was actually billionaires that funded al-Qaeda to destabilize the Middle East? Then, when our own U.S. troops began posting pictures on Facebook stating, "I will not fight alongside al-Qaeda" and, "I will not train al-Qaeda" things began to turn against some evil government planners. These soldiers had written on cardboard covering their faces (while in uniform).

Our own troops had to flat out refuse to train the same murdering scum al-Qaeda that was attacking them in Iraq. This is why the name al-Qaeda was switched to Isis. I don't like mentioning the name (because it's part of a huge sham on the public) but do enjoy revealing cheap parlor tricks to a country of marks. There's actually evidence that Harry Houdini was possibly knocked-off by fraudulent psychics that he was exposing. Mr. Houdini had actively begun discrediting crooks posing as psychics that were preying upon distraught people and claiming to contact their dead relatives (for money of course). Exposing huge frauds always runs the risk of getting whacked by one of them. To see the looks on the faces of tyrannical people when the angry mob finally understands the crimes that have been committed against them certainly sounds worth it to me.

Do you remember when President Obama and John Kerry were trying to convince (sell) the public that we had to attack Syria in 2014? As radio host Alex Jones frequently says, the architects of our government think that you're so stupid that they fund ISIS and then after ISIS attacks overseas, our own government gets to put more cameras on our streets. Due to the terror threat that our own government created, we're constantly told to surrender more rights.

The human brain can't defend against repeated lies on TV stated as the truth. When combined with alcohol, anti-depressants, and a constant drip feed of fluoride (known brain inhibitor) into our blood streams, we're turned into obedient zombies. This brain-deadening cocktail has held the public at bay for decades. New neural pathways are being created that will favor logic and truth. The result, less fear.

The wealthy have been living with increasing levels of decadence while the rest of us struggle to pay for housing, food, and gasoline. The appearance of people on television that tell us how to live and what to be thinking about isn't reality. They don't look anything like that in real life without tons of TV makeup on.

It's about time that the curtain is pulled aside to reveal the Wizard of OZ (the president) for what he really is: a small group of little old white men that have taken absolute control of what they see as an otherwise lost herd of idiots. Our doctors are guilty for throwing drugs at all of us to solve practically everything. We continue to get less and less healthy in spite of taking more and more medication (drugs). Doctors too have been bought-off by the same billionaires that own the President, the House, and the Senate. The President is merely the spokesperson and fall-guy to take the blame.

News anchors are just reading a script in the name of making $200,000 per year. If this was your existence, would you have any motivation to question the content of what you were reading? David Icke perfectly calls our TV reporters what they really are, news readers. The only thing that actually questioning their teleprompter (speech controller) will get them is a pink slip. Do you think that news readers want to lose $200,000 per year jobs and end up stuck in the trenches with $10 per hour front-line zombies?

Checkout the movie "Surrogates" with Bruce Willis. Watch it, and you'll get what spending all day stuck in front of a screen has done to most of us. The amount of youth and vitality that can be regained by abandoning TV-induced paralysis is incredible. Our group accepts or denies the world that we live in. If you want to see scary looking bloated messes on TV that have sworn allegiance to the government that bribes them $200,000 a year; then remove the caked-on makeup that hides the real people delivering us the news. They look a whole lot different without the magic of TV makeup. Even high school athletes tower over some of our favorite action heroes. Many leading men don't even prefer women. It's all an illusion.

Unhealthy people that are always covered by makeup are like a badly burned birthday cake covered in frosting. I'm not a fan of burnt-cake Americans. The little kid from "The Sixth Sense" sees dead people and so do I. When you stop following the zombie diet, you'll begin to see the difference between the living and the dead. Zombies at home would seriously consider sobering themselves up if they saw these people for an entire week with no TV makeup on. We'd be like zombies seeing our own true reflections in the mirror for the very first time.

A handful of elites that have amassed a great deal of wealth have crowned themselves kings. Unfortunately, they long ago started making decisions on behalf of the rest of us without our consent. I was once one of their hopeless zombies. Then one day, it occurred to me that I had lost self-control. I turned off my TV, started reading books and stopped copying the same routine as the least healthy Americans do.

Perhaps when my older brother with the 150+ IQ (that read books constantly in high school) stopped using fluoride toothpaste, it was for a reason. I remember being a little kid and thinking it was strange that my teenage brother was brushing his teeth with nothing but water. Perhaps he'd stumbled onto the brain handicapping effects of daily fluoride use.

What does fluoride have to do with any of this? Nazi scientists discovered that after putting a very small amount of fluoride into the drinking water (only 1-3 parts per million) at the concentration camps, that the prisoners stopped trying as hard to escape. Fluoride was proven to be an effective brain sedative. It's no wonder why your kids are being prescribed legalized speed (Ritalin) so they can pay attention in class.

Joseph Stalin also used fluoride in the drinking water in his prisons. The latest "Resident Evil" movie worked in some Russian zombies for a reason. Most scenes in movies aren't put together by mistake. Sometimes movie scenes are arranged in a subtle way so that they're directly absorbed by your sub-conscious mind. I was once told that my straight forward communication style and frankness was as subtle as a two-by-four across the side of your head. Stalin found that his government could reduce the number of prison guards by 75% after fluoride had been introduced into the inmates' water supply.

There are literally thousands of studies confirming the negative brain effects caused by fluoride ingestion. What do all Americans do twice a day every day? More amazingly, we all force our toddlers to put something in their mouths that says, "Contact poison control if product is swallowed" right on the side of the tube. We do this because we were taught to by people that we trusted. Dentists are changing their tune on fluoride. Google it.

Would politicians and billionaires introduce a daily dose of something that made us all just a little dumber without us knowing about it? Simply YouTube water fluorination and see what you find. How many super wealthy people do you think drink city water straight from their tap? Fluoride-free distilled water can make an incredible difference. A gallon of distilled water per day can transform an acidic overweight body into a healthier and slimmer you.

Parasitic politicians don't want you to become a better problem solver and self-sufficient. They would prefer that you drink diet soda, eat fast food, pay them taxes for protection (from terrorists that they sent money and guns to) and keep your mouth shut. Never mind the expensive whole house water softening systems used by many wealthy people. If thousands of dollars for clean water is simply too much for you, then what about 75 cents a day for a gallon of distilled water?

What other mammals on earth ingest fluoride to protect their teeth? Has it ever occurred to you that some of the smartest people out there may already be avoiding fluoride altogether? Other countries have outlawed public water fluorination already, yet our city leaders keep insisting on dumping fluoride into our water supply. Are the local governors and city council members more or less wealthy than you?

Why is fluoride the main ingredient in some rat poisons? We use rats to test many chemicals on, due to a similar reaction to how things affect us. German scientists figured this all out a very long time ago. Those that are truly in the know avoid using fluoride in their own food and drinking water (all while telling the voters that it's all perfectly safe). Don't question if any of this is true and don't look into it at all. Trust your loving government officials because I'm sure that they love you a lot.

We all get told the same things over and over again from the time that we're kids until it becomes fact; even if, the fact is a lie. That is until one day somebody finally comes along and exposes the lie by proving their counter arguments against it. As adults, until the majority of us are convinced otherwise, the lie continues to be known as the truth.

Are the majority of Americans really smart people? Past examples of humanity's brilliance: Santa Claus, the Easter Bunny, cigarettes are good for you, asbestos is a safe insulator, hiding under your school desk will help protect you after a nuclear blast, x-ray machines used in the early 1900's to measure shoe size are safe. We're essentially living on the planet of the apes. Unfortunately, we are the talking apes.

Our owners don't want us using past knowledge to solve our current problems. Instead, people watching the History channel are forced to watch teams of tattooed dirt bags wearing all black buying and selling junk from desperate Americans in the spiritual Mecca of Las Vegas, Nevada. A whole country of retards is very easy to manipulate.

Billionaires have bought all of the land, water and resources in this world. The problem is, the money used to buy most of it only exists in cyberspace. Forbes magazine just released a list of the world's wealthiest billionaires in 2013; there were over 400 of them. That's 400 billionaires that are walking around on planet earth right now and dominating 7 billion human beings with electronic money that's backed by nothing. There's a fascinating documentary about our money system called, "The Money Masters" explaining in detail how our banking system was founded.

A millionaire is about as important to a billionaire, as a homeless person is to the rest of us. Please picture a pile of 1 million dollar bills dumped in your front yard. Then, multiply that pile by 999 times and visualize just how much land mass that pile of loose singles would actually cover. That's the wealth of one billionaire, and it's all worthless paper backed by nothing. In fact, each billionaire doesn't even hold all of that paper; it's just a number on a computer screen. There's no vault of gold, and no big pile of paper (anywhere). Sadly, it's all just numbers on computer screens that are loaned out to marks that happen to rinse their mouths with a known neurotoxin twice daily. Cheers.

It takes the wealth of 999 millionaires to add up to the wealth of a single billionaire. So millionaires, if you want to survive the zombie apocalypse then you'd better start waking up the zombies as fast as you can. Otherwise, they'll one day be used on you, just like the Nazis were used on the wealthy Jewish people living in Socialist Germany. Human beings can be trained to blindly follow orders, no matter how insane those orders are. This has been proven in recent history. To think that the American public (that we all consider not-so-bright as a whole) is any less susceptible to conforming to a nasty dictatorship is a comfortable lie. The blinders are being taken off now so that we don't repeat history. To the establishment's horror, the public is awakening.

Videos of police brutality in the U.S. right now, in the year 2015 ought to be enough for you to put aside your favorite toothpaste and try something new. I was handcuffed in front of a gas station in February of 2014 because I had the same short haircut as some ghetto thug that they were looking for (brown short hair, white guy). After spending a few heart-pounding minutes in cuffs and completely surrounded by cops, the head detective made it all ok by telling me, "The good news is, that we're taking the cuffs off." After that, they let me go so that I could enter the gas station and purchase two bottles of non-fluorinated water. For zombies that don't realize what deep shit we're all in as a nation, this ought to make you unplug your cable box right now. Mindless troops blindly following absurd orders already have a massive presence on U.S. soil.

Which houses and pantries are still going to have food in them if cornered politicians cut-off the food supply of 100 million zombies on food stamps and social security? Have you ever faced an army of hungry people that's 100 million strong? There aren't enough guns and bullets to win a war against those numbers. Countries are conquered with words, not guns. The zombies will always win. In 2014, I was detained like a farm animal for the crime of faintly resembling a white guy with a short hair cut. Looking at my face and speaking to me for thirty seconds was simply too risky for a half dozen heavily-armed police officers.

If there's one thing that rich people get, it's eliminating their competition. If you have 500 million bucks and your competition has one million, (but better ideas than you) would they use a bunch of brainless zombies to haul competitors away after making up lies about them on TV? History has already answered this question. The Ministry Of Truth in "1984" did the same thing. We have the nightly news. Public opinion is very easy to mold. Unfortunately, it's the richest men in the world that are broadcasting reality.

People like Bill Cosby can be destroyed overnight. In reality, the general public has no idea whether or not Mr. Cosby is really guilty of the accused crimes. He may be, but we're simply going from details offered to us all from the same media that says the economy has improved since 2008 while food stamp recipients continue to increase to an incredible 50 million Americans in 2015. If Mr. Cosby is guilty of the horrific accusations against him, this only confirms that public images of powerful people can be white-washed for decades (White Water).

Waking up the brains of our neighbors is the key to our group's survival. Our military and police are good men that mean well. The vast majority of all police, military, and civil servants are good people. Please help unplug them before you get handcuffed first and identified later. This really did happen to me and could happen to any one of you reading this. It did happen during the rise of the Nazis and in Socialist Russia (the USSR). Brute force supported by mobs of idiots could repeat if a Socialist America was brought about.

How smart are the citizens that would apply for jobs serving Homeland Security to enforce more rules on the rest of us? How blindly would some of these people follow orders? There are documented experiments where people had very little problem electrocuting other people, so long as they were given the order. Google it.

We know what a great track record human beings in positions of power have regarding telling the truth to the people they rule over. As in, they make the rules that you and I have to live by, but they don't. Does that sound about right? How long must this go on before decent people start reasoning with their neighbors? Good people will follow bad orders if they're on the zombie diet.

If I woke up one day only to realize that I was a slow stupid zombie, by God I would find a fast smart zombie and start doing exactly what they do. The movie "Warm Bodies" explains the zombie metaphor perfectly. Helping other people around us and feeling empathy for them is the key to our survival. The human heart can do amazing things. When triggered, our hearts release a tremendous source of energy that evil men can do nothing about. Whether you know it or not, this book is opening up connections that will get your heart pumping again and restore connections in your brain. We all know that feeling of intense love and the courage that it gives us. When you love something, you'll demonstrate bravery to defend it. When you truly love something, you're willing to die defending it.

If you believe in God, then perhaps all of the zombie movies have been God's subtle attempt to reason with us. An attempt from God to show us what we're becoming, (in an over exaggerated fashion) so that we can reject it. Does that make sense? Millionaires that have 30 years left to live need to realize that young idiots pose a huge threat. Being a zombie is very much reversible. All that we have to do is decide to unplug from the daily TV programming and stop sedating ourselves all to hell. We have no problem at all looking at other people's beliefs in foreign countries and pointing out that some of their beliefs are insane. To this day there are countries that sexually mutilate women and forbid them from driving cars. Handcuffing the wrong person without questioning them first is a bad sign for America.

Any outside observer can easily see the harm being done to us, but we're blind to it. It's not fun to accept that we've been deceived, but too many other people are sounding the alarm. Perhaps it's finally time that you investigate a little. As you do, you'll likely see that more of this book will ring true than you ever could have imagined. Massive attacks using racial division in the mainstream media are already happening in 2015. The goal is to divide and conquer working-class people, start riots, bring in troops, and then roll out more controlling forms of governance. Paris, France recently had a mass shooting involving Muslim terrorists. Afterward there were troops on their streets and discussions of a curfew. World bankers have worldwide long-term strategies in place.

We need to begin abandoning convenient fairy tales that have been sold to us by our honest politicians. Billionaires want you drinking daily because you're much easier to screw over without any retaliation. Deep down inside, drunks know that they're drunks. Potheads on the other hand, don't know that they're potheads. Soma is real, and it's working. We're like millions upon millions of cowardly lions just waiting for someone else to come along and hand us some courage.

Dorothy just showed up, and you're reading her book. Only her is a him, or she is a he, or something like that. Courage is being installed right now. By the end of this book, ballsier you will be. Imagine our corrupt politicians freaking-out because a software update for cowardly voters (making them brave) has finally been created. Freaking-out politicians and a fearless public laughing in their faces is a scenario God would applaud.

Try going without any sedatives for an entire month and you tell me if you're not smarter, braver, and don't have a better working memory. People that ingest coffee after 5pm and are surprised that they need sleeping pills (a pill-form of alcohol) are wrecking their memory. If you stop taking these brain numbing pills or drinks before bed every night, then your memory will begin to improve. How are we supposed to solve problems if our memory is shot?

Young people don't respect old people that can't operate a dvd player; nor do politicians and billionaires respect drunken adults that can't legally drive a car. At the very end of the remade "1984" movie, the character Winston found himself locked up in an institution. The defeated slave readily accepts his daily shots of gin with a few drops of some chemical added to it that seems to keep him hopeless and docile. The authorities had also trained Winston to accept and repeat that 2+2=5, showing that with enough repetition all logic can be abandoned. Common Core.

Even bold lies can easily be accepted as the truth (by people that sedate themselves daily). There are also constant alcohol commercials on TV that remind you to sedate yourself (just in case you'd forgotten). The message is repeated to all of us that still watch TV no less than 100 times per day. If you want to see real live zombies at the grocery store, then stop sedating yourself for an entire month. Slow moving zombies in the movies were no mistake.

Chapter 9 – Ugly Truths

Believing that jet airplanes crashing into buildings causes the steel-framed structures to implode into a giant pile of dust is just as ridiculous as saying that 2+2=5. To not research 911 Truth is to betray the founding fathers of this country and everybody else that died under the false pretenses of the 911 attacks. Three buildings in New York City were demolished that day, not two. Fires inside of steel and concrete buildings don't make them implode. Ever.

Infantile adults are preventing the rest of us from explaining the 911 magicians trick to the rest of the non-retarded group members. Some of you have the intelligence to perceive when you're dealing with a sharp person, and some of you don't. At some point, the sharpest people in America need to stand up at town hall meetings and lay their reputations on the line by speaking the truth in front of large crowds (of not-so-bright people).

Donald Rumsfeld was telling Congress that two trillion dollars was missing on the day before 911. The two trillion dollars wasn't spoken of again following the 911 attacks that occurred the very next morning. How convenient for Mr. Rumsfeld and the presidential administration at that time. Look and see if this is a verifiable and factual statement.

Life hasn't been easy for those of us that have had to work for a living since 911. That was the beginning of a rapid decline in the net worth of average Americans. Having the additional stress of the 911 attacks on top of the normal problems of working-class people was simply too much for many sober adults to handle. So, what did many of us start doing more of as the US economy has slowly eroded away? Only a few years after 911, Weapons of Mass Distraction were shipped into the US in the form of flat screen TVs. I don't care who you are, you'd have to be a robot not to get seduced by a brand new 50" flat screen in your family room. I know I did. Cable TV+50" flatscreen+daily alcohol or weed=American zombie.

The now critical nature of our present economy (not only in the USA, but worldwide) calls for us to pull it together. We've become a country of drunken pill-popping sheep being led to the slaughter by wolves in suits. The thing is, when we're unplugged from all of the routine public handicaps, we suddenly become able to stand our ground with the wolves. We must help one another to sober up and turn off our TVs because they've robbed us of our speed and strength. It's time to restore sanity as a country because our survival as a group now depends upon it.

We must start holding ourselves accountable for our own selfish actions and start helping our neighbors. If the whole country goes down I've got news for you, you'll be living in the mess. Then, all of those zombie apocalypse movies will make perfect sense (way too late). We don't have to go down that road and I don't think we will. Our billionaire elites that have been terrifying all of us for the last 10 years have taken too much too fast. Millions of former middle-classers are done with being afraid.

We're all constantly asked to ignore our God-given consciences just to get by. Over the course of a lifetime we've been conditioned to be cold and heartless toward other people. Do you think that it might be time to start listening to that conscience that tells you to do what's right? When we finally break our mental chains of addiction, fear-based control systems (that only empower the wealthy) will crumble. We'll finally raise our level of consciousness and start saying no when wealthier sociopaths are making unreasonable demands upon us.

We'll naturally know the difference between right and wrong, and do what's right more often. Not, what's convenient, or what will appease wealthier jerks standing in front of us and making threats. Stop living under rules and conditions that our leaders don't follow themselves. The whole slave and master relationship can be ended. After unplugging yourself from the same brain drains as the other zombies, something amazing will begin to happen. Strangers from all over will begin listening to you. Your words alone will carry more power because you'll look and feel better than the other docile people all around you. Sincerity goes a long way, along with friendliness that goes along with self-respect.

Each day as I'm adding the final touches to this book, more and more people are engaging in conversations about formerly forbidden topics. To regain our God-given conscience is to regain the highest level of freedom available here on earth. Dictators on earth know this and are throwing everything that they can at the public. Greedy politicians prefer a fearful public. When the public stops following the slow zombie diet, it'll be checkmate. They don't think it can happen, but I do. More primitive versions of this book have already helped others before you break free from bad situations.

When it comes to our high-level government officials, (and the banking executives that own them) we outnumber them by nearly a million to one. That's one million (currently sedated) cattle-like people for every one wolf-like politician. How on earth in a republic haven't we fired all of the corrupt officials already?

In "1984" George Orwell perfectly illustrated the tremendous threat that television poses to the masses when utilized by government. It's fair to say that Mr. Orwell was ahead of his time. He saw that future tools of indoctrination would transform previously intelligent citizens into primitive child-like adults.

Go online and find the movie "Conquest of The Planet of The Apes". Watch that movie trailer and then ask yourself, are the contrasting lives of upper and lower class Americans really that different? Do you notice that heavily armed police are used in the movie to defend the owner-class from their slightly less intelligent servant-class?

Most Americans have become little more than well-trained and TV-programmed servants to the wealthy. The rich stay rich (and don't work at all) and most of us continue kissing their asses and groveling to them for crumbs just like the servant apes in the movie that I won't shut up about: "Conquest of The Planet of The Apes." When a conquest has been completed, you end up with a bunch of poor and pathetic people.

The most comfortable Americans are those in the decadent ruling class or those cheating the welfare system. As long as a retiree is receiving a Social Security check, they'll accept full-blown tyranny for working-aged Americans without making a sound. Social Security checks were an ingenious short-term plan to pacify 1/3 of the population while America is openly dismantled and conquered.

Elites of the world simply weren't satisfied with having cats, dogs and pathetic spouses to completely dominate for a lifetime, they want more. When the world bankers pulled the plug on the U.S. economy in 2008, they made a stupendous mistake. They left alive millions of people like us walking around their newly formed prison without bars. The prison is so high tech that the bars are merely mental. Much like in "The Shawshank Redemption", it didn't take long for old Andy to walk through the prison unmolested by the other inmates or guards.

The internet that was likely designed to monitor and police us all has instead become an impossible-to-stop spread of information. Low-level people are now exposing high-level scams. The truth resonates with people. Lies and corruption are being exposed daily at an ever-accelerating pace worldwide.

Orwell knew that with well-planned propaganda that corrupt leaders would manipulate the masses with ease. Billionaires own all of the TV stations and have the final say of everything that we're allowed to see. The propaganda is beginning to fail. As far as we're told, the teachings of a dude named Jesus Christ got him crucified by the Roman government (alongside of a couple of other revolutionaries). Back then it was only one enlightened man and a small group of disciples that quickly disbanded when things got ugly. Now, there are millions upon millions of God-fearing people exposing corruption all over the world.

Jesus had flawless logic (just like Spock) and a large conscience that the Roman government couldn't corrupt with money. Truly heightened consciousness gives even the common man a set of brass balls. So, they had to kill him to stop the spread of an enlightened way of thinking (heightened consciousness) to the masses. Regular people were starting to listen to him (in spite of the fact that he didn't have any money).

You can't have a reasonable person that's able to point out the flawed logic in a corrupt system walking around and removing fear from the common man. Our organized religions have been infiltrated and corrupted as well. Pastors of mega-churches are corporately friendly and politically correct (while their congregations become poorer and poorer). Preachers mentioning Isis every Sunday ought to raise red flags. What does God care about Isis? Sell-out preachers that have taken dirty government money to avoid this brutal job market won't escape the karmic hammer that universal law promises them.

When is the majority (that does believe in some sort of God) going to stop following the orders of men who keep getting caught lying to us? They don't even believe in simply being good. Yet, we keep allowing them to set the rules over the rest of us. We pretend that they are God-fearing people while their actions and their bank accounts tell another story. Saintly leaders don't need 100 million dollars of personal assets (especially if they're spreading a Socialist philosophy). Is Hillary Clinton going to donate all of her money to the working poor? Don't hold your breath.

The masses have to stand up in numbers to dishonest men and women. If only one person jumps off the ground in a sports stadium, nothing happens. However, if fifty thousand people all jump off the ground at the same time, the whole stadium shakes. Will crooks take swings and a few shots at an awakened public? Yes, ensuring their arrests and removal from power. It's worth it. Let our scummy politicians and bankers lash out at the public for broadcasting the truth.

Politicians have been caught red handed for millennia taking advantage of their power and ignoring the well-being of their tax base. It's time for this to stop (and for humanity to evolve spiritually). Do you get why dictators wouldn't want the masses to obtain true spirituality? We've all been postponing some very necessary confrontations in our lives. Do you want to end up like millions of dirt poor Chinese factory workers that avoid confrontation at all costs? Are they free?

Once your conscience has been boosted and your brain has had corrupt programs eliminated from it, a stronger and more spiritual connection becomes possible. This is more so your own personal journey to getting connected to all that's good within you. Organized churches still have plenty of customers that seem to have no conscience left at all. Nearly all of our churches stay locked up and empty six days a week. This proves that helping the needy is a bottom priority for all of those beautiful and empty buildings. Those churches could be housing the homeless and feeding the needy. There's a clear difference between boosting consciousness and being religious.

A lot of happy people that have raised their level of consciousness did so by tackling their own addictions. They turned off their TV and stopped seeing everyone else as separate. We're on this ride together. Finding common ground and happy mediums is a good place to start. We share the same land, water, and air with each other. Once your own inner spirituality gets turned back on again, fear, hatred, and greed just seem to melt away. They get replaced with more tolerance, patience, generosity, and increased empathy for mankind.

We can even forgive world elites that currently own everything. We just don't have to keep them in charge of all of us any longer. If flesh and blood people are acting shamefully toward a large group, then the group is allowed to defend itself. If you've been sucked into the insanity of addiction like I once was, it's ok, it happens to the best of us. Life is meant to be lived and we can't learn without making lots of mistakes. When we find ourselves totally lost, beat down, and defeated, for God's sake surrender. Not to evil men, but to God. Not to politicians claiming to serve God, but to your own good conscience.

Admit that your way isn't working anymore, lay your pride aside, and admit total defeat to God and ask for help. Prayer does help but must be followed by positive actions. Help will come from other people that have recovered from similar circumstances. They do exist, and there are tons of them out there. The peace that's unleashed after sobering up, telling the truth to others is a profound experience. Going at life alone is a terrible and painful strategy. There are literally billions of people sharing this planet. Each new kind act toward a stranger makes looking into the mirror a little easier. It feels really good to help strangers.

Love for other people (and humanity in general) is the greatest gift that God has put into this experience. Nothing in a bottle, no pill, and no drug can outdo the awesome power of love. Like a giant tidal wave in the ocean, love can level any man, woman or child. Or, it can transport us straight into heaven on earth. Love is a wave that I've ridden several times. I'll continue trying to catch the next wave until the day this body stops breathing. That's my hope. If you're not here on earth to love other people, then what are you doing here?

Our human brains may never fully be able to comprehend what God and love truly are. I'm thinking that little kids can probably do a better job teaching us about God and love than our TV sets, preachers, and politicians have done thus far. All I see on TV is that alcohol and pills will duct-tape our soulless corpses back together just enough to keep going back to that horrible job that you endure, so you can buy the stuff you don't need, and continue on in relationships that are making you so happy that you have trouble facing them without daily sedation.

Abusive boyfriends, girlfriends, and spouses are really going to love this book! For all truly shitty relationships, this book is the beginning of the end. When consciousness gets raised, abusive relationships get ended. There will be short periods of uncomfortable change followed by long lasting fulfillment and relief. Consciousness gives people a combination of courage, brains, and restraint not to unnecessarily harm others.

We all deserve to be treated with respect and dignity now, today, here on earth and during this lifetime. Only parasitic people (that want countries full of cowardly slaves) would train (former) middle-class citizens (that do follow the rules) to suffer terribly today for future promises tomorrow (that never come true). Why would God want the most honest and faithful people to suffer the most while here?

The most common thing about sociopaths claiming to be religious is that they are always making you future promises that never come true. In the meantime, they need your time, your energy, and some of your money. Our moral leaders live in bigger houses, have larger bank accounts, drive nicer cars, and eat more expensive meals than you. Their kids get to attend expensive schools and get better jobs while your weekly offering pays for it all. I think that God got cut out of the deal. George Carlin had a very similar bit.

It's not that Mr. Carlin was pissed-off at God, just at our gullible congregations and the greedy preachers that gladly fleece them. Most of these preachers need to start using their empty churches to house the homeless and feed the poor. Churches could quickly end food stamp dependency nationwide. There are a lot of upper-middle-class churches in America that have entire congregations claiming to be anti-government handout. Put your money where your mouth is and as Jesus says, help thy neighbor. People that love money, typically don't.

The financially comfortable people that control these organized religions follow none of the rules. Fat selfish religious people that live like kings now while their neighbors slave away for 50 hrs a week (while in poverty) aren't fooling God. A church person with no self-control is still powerless over their addictions (including money) no matter how many times they mention the name Jesus Christ. If Christ and the angels do return, they're going to hand out a beating to fat church people with shiny new cars.

Millions of honest Americans are working full-time and living in total poverty. Churches have merely been an ego-masturbation for selfish human beings to believe that they're decent. Churches across the country have been reduced to a guilt-relieving mechanism. Truly Christ-like Americans are actually living in poverty while working constantly and sharing with those that need help. Church peoples' lack of generosity has resulted in 50 million food stamp recipients. Apparently the government is God.

After the big crash of 2008, the American dream has turned into the American nightmare. For many still suffering, the only exceptions are those brief escapes from reality via drug and alcohol induced stupors. Millions of Americans have lost their jobs, houses, and can barely afford food and gasoline to commute to jobs that have only gotten harder and don't pay enough to live on.

The nationwide unemployment rate is supposedly at less than 6%. What a huge joke that statistic is. We all know that the true nationwide unemployment rate is much closer to 20% and isn't improving. Good people that have always attempted to follow the golden rule aren't immune to the traps of addiction in this post 2008 economy.

The same billionaires that created the financial collapse are now selling the public (that they see as nothing more than trainable primates) a barrage of drugs, alcohol, and lies via TV. They want to keep the entire herd distracted, confused, overwhelmed and docile while the American dream circles the toilet bowl. Billionaires would rather eliminate us and open up the borders to provide cheap third-world slave labor than do what's right. In the elites eyes we're like an increasingly uppity heard of cattle.

20% unemployment, no problem, let's bring in 30 million more unemployed people from south of the border. I'd rather spread upper-class logic to third-world people. Let's ruin our potential replacements worldwide by educating third-world people with sound logic and the belief in workers' rights. It can be done.

When you turn the word God around backwards, you end up with the word Dog. People will only allow themselves to be treated like dogs after they've lost all spirituality. They may be religious, but large groups of people living under tyrannical governance certainly aren't brave. Sometimes multitudes of smart people develop the same problems due to a terrible economy. During the Great Depression millions of people died of malnutrition and health problems that go along with being poor and frequently drunk. It's time to start helping ourselves.

Global elites have no problem watching former middle-class Americans self-destruct. My response is to refuse self-administered euthanasia and to begin fixing broken Americans as fast as possible. I've been known to fix things and always seem to make them go just a little faster. There's great value in both old machines and in older people. For the most part, a few common parts become clogged-up over the course of time. A 200 Horsepower vehicle can sit for too long and be deemed worthless by upper-class Americans (or Millennials) that can't fix anything (and always buy new). Resourcefulness has great value. Rather than working 50 hours per week at two low-paying jobs, (leaving the worker drained) average Americans can gain intelligence and begin fixing their own problems.

Many of you reading this will quickly tell me that you've gotten too old and it's too late. While reading, I've already taken apart your vehicle, cleaned out an old carburetor that was completely clogged and am putting things back together again. I've also removed the power robbing governor. It turns out that it was just put in there so you'd keep accepting the next round of well-crafted lies delivered every four years (while you get older and poorer).

There's an account of Abraham Lincoln visiting Charleston, South Carolina just after the civil war had ended and the slaves had been freed. While President Lincoln was walking through the streets, a black man bowed down to Mr. Lincoln and without hesitation President Lincoln bowed back to the black man. Honest Abe told the former slave, "You don't need to bow down before any man, only bow down before God." Imagine Morgan Freeman's voice saying, "You damn right!"

We must bring ourselves to admit that our government and financial system are both totally corrupted and operated by the same small minority of criminals. They want us all to bow down to them (and to our own personal addictions) and become their servants. For those of us who want actual positive change, we must stop doing the same things daily. We must communicate to our friends, family and neighbors about the lies that we've remained in denial about. Political correctness is conforming to corruption.

Things in the U.S. won't get any better until we face the truth together. Our manipulators only exist for as long as we continue seeing our neighbors as our enemies. We're all better than this. We must come to believe that hundreds of millions of Americans (and billions of people around the world) can have rewarding lives that are governed by love, logic, and common sense. Not just my country, my race, my religion, or myself.

It's ok if we've gotten lost along the way during the ride of life. We must learn from our mistakes and quit doing what's no longer working. Millionaires often forget that their decisions to make them more money are hurting real people. Deep down, most people are good. It's only the TV that's programmed people to believe and behave otherwise. When that powerful mind altering device is unplugged, you'll be amazed at how much better you'll begin to feel.

We must renegotiate a more mutually beneficial relationship for our group. Sociopaths only behave in a certain way for as long as the people around them allow it. Once we confront them, they'll generally attack or run. Our fear of confrontation is what can perpetuate a lifetime of misery. Once we've tackled personal demons, it's much harder for others to dominate us.

Removing TV, drinking only distilled water, using non-fluoride toothpaste and flushing out bowels filled with years of processed foods will begin to allow fresh fuel to reach your brain. The difference between a barely-running vehicle and a beast of a classic is a needle-sized hole in each carburetor (supplying gas to your engine). All you need to do now is start putting in good fuel and you'll be amazed. Mental walls that were put in place by our societal controllers are now gone. Your very own processor is now coming to more logical conclusions that will directly benefit you.

Chapter 10 – Taking Back Our Power

The true power is (and always has been) at the bottom of the pyramid. We've simply been tricked, trained, drugged-up and fed cheap drinks to not realize this. A relative handful of wealthy men have made us believe that they hold all of the power. They don't. In fact, they never have. It's always been nothing more than a well orchestrated illusion.

We need to realize that we are indeed spiritual beings that have no reason to fear death. To make life better for the majority, we must not fear losing our lives while fighting for the freedom of our group. Kings and politicians have feared the enlightenment of the masses for thousands of years. They know that if the masses all get really smart, then we'll see no need for protection.

Some people will sacrifice us all for more money. Why not dust yourself off like old Harrison Ford and punch out a few Nazi offspring before you die. Thousands of Nazis did come to the U.S. following World War II via Operation Paperclip. They then became U.S. citizens and were absorbed right into the military industrial complex that President Eisenhower warned about when he left office. Congress and our President all answer indirectly to the same group of globally reaching corporations and billionaires that own them.

Why is it that the majority of U.S. citizens are now being ignored and experiencing a declining quality of life? At the exact same time a minority of billionaires are making all of the rules that govern our ever-worsening lives. Good people are being dictated to and we all know it. This is a spineless way to continue existing.

We must take back our power and realize that we determine the fate of our own lives (not a few wealthy sociopaths with zero concern for the group). Our sheer numbers can't be beaten when working together. Every zombie movie ever made illustrates this point. The numbers always win. Whatever direction that we the zombies decide to go, we go.

Other people have been steering us, and it's time that we start steering ourselves again. Everyone reading this is gaining a greater level of self-control. The power to create a more positive timeline for your own life has already been increased. Multiple power supply wires to your brain that had been cut by the controllers of our society (via TV programming) have now been repaired.

Stop watching TV and you're cutting the control cord between you and the manipulators of our declining society. Each time you plop down in front of your TV, you'll quickly re-clog your freshly cleaned-out processor (and remain a non-threat zombie to the world banking elites). Keep your TV off and refuse to pay attention to it. The additional brain power from the repair work that's already been done will become obvious over the course of time.

Why is raising the consciousness of the average American so extremely vital? Well, we are kind of getting our asses kicked as a group. 50 million Americans receiving food assistance is not exactly a sign of a healthy economy. If you're fat and happy and really don't care about those other people, then you'll change your mind real quick when their food stamps get cut off in a final attempt to kickoff a new civil (civilian) war. We're not going to let this happen. You now have the will to refuse the things that have artificially lowered the brain-power of the ignorant masses.

If the path to obtaining these things simply starts with unplugging your cable cord and refusing to pay attention to TV wherever you go, will you try it? There's a reason that both Neo and Morpheus in the original "Matrix" movie are standing in front of a TV (with a big pyramid on the back of it). Can you believe the paper-thin electrical wire of control that surrounds our belief systems?

We're like 300 million cattle returning to jobs that we hate and spending lifetimes in fear due to just one little electrical wire going into the back of a voluntary (government-approved) hypnosis machine. The same wire might as well be plugged into the back of your head. How many cattle (awaiting slaughter) will remain in the field when a few small electrical wires separating them from freedom are turned off?

They must first see a cow breach the fence without getting shocked. When the other cows realize that the fence has been turned off, (and have gained knowledge of the upcoming slaughter) it doesn't take long for a stampede to form. Do you want to be one of the American food stamp army? I don't. The more that we rely on others to provide us food and shelter, the more control they can exert over our lives.

Isn't it about time that we stop doing what everybody else in a suffering herd is also doing every day? Unplugging your TV is like unplugging the electrical fence. All this time our completely corrupt control system has been hanging by a paper-thin wire. The all-seeing eye can simply be unplugged.

Repeating the same daily routine as 50 million food stamp cattle isn't a good idea anymore. Stalin amassed an army of citizens on food stamps too. It wasn't a good time for that group. We don't need to repeat what the socialist Russians did because we can learn from their past mistakes. I don't want to be huddled in a cold room sharing one potato with my entire family. That type of nonsense was accepted by an entire country of people (not that long ago). All, while those same citizens were told that unemployment was dropping and production numbers were rising. Billions of people are now living in poverty rather than standing up to their oppressors. Everyone reading this now knows how to cut the electrified fence that's been protecting our loving politicians, bankers and 1% from the zombies.

Our TV sets and smart-phones have all been used to shock our psyches to keep us in line. Watching buildings implode on 911 was the ultimate shock. Afterwards, we all readily accepted cattle-like treatment of ourselves at airports and in our homes. Suddenly our phone calls are listened to and our emails are swept for suspicious words. This is no different than what Russian citizens dealt with under Stalin's control. Everything there was watched and listened to, just as it is here and now. In the meantime, corrupt officials live like kings.

We literally allow ourselves to be corralled, searched, and processed just like criminals within our own country. The makers of "V For Vendetta" (released in 2006) had a pretty damn good crystal ball to describe present day problems. The movie mentions Muslims, Immigrants, Sexuality, and shows what our beloved news anchors look like when you look behind the curtain. All fiction of course, but used to tell the truth. As stated in the movie, "Words will always retain their power" and my personal favorite, "Ideas are bulletproof."

Many of us continue to repeat ridiculous premises like: 911was pulled off by guys with box cutters, NORAD just happened to have a full stand-down that same day, and the buildings weren't demolished using a controlled demolition. Somehow people actually believe all of these statistically impossible coincidences occurring on the same day. The electrical fence surrounding the field of your mind has been cut, its power is off and you don't have to plug it back in.

Zombies are also oblivious to the fact that the Supreme Court has granted corporations equal value as a person. This is mass insanity suffered by a mass population that was victimized by a massive Psy-Op. As in, a psychological operation carried off by a third party (not bearded guys in caves that practice crossing monkey bars). Only a planet full of talking apes would buy such a rubbish story. With satellites, drones, and electronic surveillance technology, all of the actual terrorists on earth could be killed in a week. They're just kept around to keep the public in need of protection (so that bureaucrats can avoid heavy lifting alongside of the proles).

Sure our politicians are super honest with everything else, but on this one issue of 911 I refuse to accept this group's consensus of reality for any longer. Our politicians created the TSA, the Patriot Act, and Obamacare. We're dealing with very classy individuals that really love us a lot. They'd never lie to us in order to exert total control over the group (while making tons of money during the process).

As of June of 2013, the Supreme Court has overturned an amendment to our constitution (that was part of the civil rights movement) to guarantee equal voting rights in all states for minorities. In other words, if states now want to implement totally racist voting registration rules, they now legally can. Perhaps old white people are about to lose their ability to vote in the next big election (should have shared those socialist security checks). Comfortable middle-class senior citizens are notoriously bad tippers to the working-poor that now serve them.

It's called karma old racist white folks. Looks like 30 million immigrants from Mexico are about to start voting for new laws that support death panels for old people. No expensive medical procedures for old people, and free healthcare for poor foreigners. Obamacare. I guess hiring the cheapest lawn crew with a whole team of illegal immigrants (rather than paying Jimmy from next door a fair wage) is finally coming around to bite you.

Smug old men collecting their Socialist Security checks frequently tell me, "I'd hate to be your age, you're screwed!" don't quite see the chess board that I do. Bill Gates is on video stating that one less old person having an expensive medical procedure could mean ten more teachers getting jobs. With 50% of current college graduates living at home with their parents, voting away old people's rights in the name of job creation won't be a stretch. Soylent Green.

It's all about going green. The lobotomized 25-35 year-olds are only concerned about inheriting grandpa's old Gran Torino (while living at their parents house and working for $10 an hour at Starbucks). The chessboard is grand. CNN and Fox News have merely been effective pacifiers for seniors. New Obamacare protocols are already being implemented by old peoples' insurance companies nationwide. Too old, sorry elderly Americans, you're insurance has denied coverage for that procedure. That's what the computer is telling the obedient doctors, nurses, and assistants reading the screens. It's all been automated, and people making good money give zero shits about the orders prescribed on the screens they're reading. Does that make sense?

Old people in America today are equally in as much danger as Jews in Germany just before young Nazis began loading them onto trains. I've lived in Florida for a few years now. The old people here are as happy as clams to live like kings while slave-like wages are all that are offered to the (faster and stronger) people now serving them. Old people greatly underestimate the complete lack of empathy present in TV-hypnotized young adults. I can just see TV-trained 25-35 year-olds (previously unemployed) loading up the trains to haul off old people to FEMA camps for $14 an hour (while texting). All the chess pieces are in place.

Both the young and the old are being set up for disaster. The concentration camps for non-party supporters won't have bars though. Instead, TV-programmed elderly are unconsciously walking themselves into hospitals and are being processed by unconscious hospital workers that are now blindly following new Obamacare (anti-senior) protocols. Each next round of flu shots contains mercury in them. If only the actual preservative didn't really have toxic metals in it, but it does. Mercury dissolves neurons.

Granted, our elderly are far too proud to unplug their TVs and far too fearful to stop administering their own daily tranquilizers. The roads sure would become safer and traffic sure would move faster. If you don't want to participate in a world that the architects of Obamacare are building, then please unplug yourself now. Remove TV programming from your operating system, and you'll begin to see things that weren't apparent before.

Both Republicans and Democrats are standing aside to let the powers-that-be legalize 30 million third world people. These new Americans can start voting with all of the superior logic and bargaining abilities that their former third-world country has taught them. The elderly wanted cheap labor today and forgot that they may be voting away your rights tomorrow. Tomorrow is here, and you're still alive. The old can start sharing with the young, and the young can refuse to support death panels. We can actually take care of one another. Let's not be divided and conquered.

Fear of public ridicule is a tremendously powerful mechanism. It has prevented the public from figuring out the massive scams that have been successfully pulled off on us all. If you say something to a friend, family member or co-worker that differs from the televised version of the story, (version of reality that all politicians support) you're likely going to get called a conspiracy theorist (thought criminal). Doesn't that term have a negative connotation? How about calling something a massive public screw-over, would that be more believable?

The super wealthy want you to stay in line with the accepted beliefs of the other zombies that will automatically attack you for threatening their existing belief systems. The programmers of the zombie public must find this to be hilarious when watching a smart and loving person get yelled at for saying something intelligent to a hypnotized person. This happens on a daily basis here in the United States just like it once did in socialist Russia and in socialist Germany. Remember, it took troops on the streets and brute force to create a socialist state. There's already an army of dependant Americans ready to give socialism a try.

Citizens that live in top-down and oppressive dictatorships worldwide do exist today; they're demoralized people that lack the will to resist a nasty existence. Until a person is snapped out of it, they cannot be reasoned with by their neighbors and will actually defend the dictator in their own country. That kind of nonsense is being wiped from your hard drive right now.

How is it that citizens become demoralized without being aware of it? Over the course of time, intelligent people just start drinking more often to prevent themselves from actually saying something smart (and getting attacked for it). This definitely happened to me in Cleveland, Ohio when I attempted to bring up the third New York City skyscraper that was demolished on 911. After commenting that his shirt was missing the third building demolished that day, a friend of mine wearing a memorial to the twin towers quickly went into attack mode.

The once friendly fireman that had always greeted me with a smile quickly turned on me. He yelled at me, "Don't you get started with that shit!" pointing his finger at me with rage in his eyes. All of our past positive interactions had been thrown out the window and the once kind man had been replaced by a programmed attack dog. Maybe he thought that armored cops wearing riot gear were going to storm into the bar and pepper-spray him in the face for even being part of such a conversation.

The otherwise kind fireman was defending which version of reality, the government-approved version or the critical thinker's? It was a sobering experience (experienced by a sober me). This is likely how it was for Germans questioning Hitler's version of reality as the Nazis slowly rose to power. The people had been hypnotized, and it was very hard to break through their programming. Could this happen in a country full of people (that in all other instances) we call morons?

Billionaires want you repeating all of the normal daily behaviors that have gotten America into our present physical, mental and spiritual health (sad state as a group). We're becoming cheap labor that can't negotiate for ourselves. Look for a rich politician to negotiate for you, because poor-people looking to a rich guy to negotiate higher wages isn't the stupidest belief on earth. To them, you're asleep, unaware, unawake, and totally unconscious of their manipulation of you. The billionaires owning America want fearful primates that follow orders with blind obedience.

John Carpenter made a movie called "They Live" featuring Rowdy Roddy Piper. It's not exactly the "Shawshank Redemption" but the movie does have a very relevant message to it. They (billionaires) live, while you sleep. You're simply a pawn on the chess board of life that sociopathic elites completely control. There's a five minute excerpt from "They Live" featured on Youtube that illustrates the main point of the movie. It's very relevant to today's economic and spiritual conditions around the world.

If we boost our own level of consciousness, then the blinders for seeing the world are taken off. There are some very true statements made in this short movie snippet that deserve five minutes of your attention. It's gravely important to understand that the tiny minority of billionaires that have bought off our politicians don't care about the well-being of the masses. With the incredible amount of worldwide land, water, advancing technology, and sunlight, how is it that starvation is still an issue?

As the elites see it, the cheaper the available worldwide labor pool gets, the better. Working-class Americans are getting beaten into the emerging worldwide (poor-peoples') labor pool. Screw your family, your friends, and your kids, all in the name of their personal profits. Universal law allows them to slaughter us if we lack the will to save ourselves.

Do you really think that going from a 26" tube TV in 1995, to a 50" flat screen in 2010 is going to decrease the amount of time that we spend consumed by a box in our homes? My own father still fails to free himself. That flat screen TV that's hooked up to a (one-way) cable box is like a radio-active vase in our family room that slowly steals our health. We can't see the damage being done, but it was put there by our enemy and our time is being stolen by it. Life goes fast. Don't let a one-way communication device steal four hours per day.

The results are astounding when we finally break free from the exact same daily behaviors that have moved the American sheeple into a complete state of apathy. The elites may be doing just fine, but we've been beaten senseless. As economies worsen, people act more primitive. The current world elites don't just want anything, they want everything. Nothing will ever be enough for them.

Worldwide governance, population control, and control of all land (to be enjoyed exclusively by the elites) while a slave-class is slowly migrated into over-populated cities is the goal. The elites will of course have mansions in the vast unpopulated tracts of wilderness. Agenda 21 is the precise name to be implemented in all countries and enforced by the United Nations worldwide.

People that actually have done research regarding Agenda 21 understand that the "Hunger Games" books and movies are a desperate attempt to show the zombie public the future world that's

122

already been planned out for us. Many writers use fiction to tell ugly truths while covering their own butts with plausible deniability. I've always preferred going straight for the jugular.

Have you been to walmartpeople.com yet? Isn't it about time that we get some tiny smidgen of self-respect back for ourselves? If you take some of these people on television out of their expensive suits and remove the caked on makeup, then some of them deserve no more credibility than Walmart people. Take away the suit, the hair, the makeup, and the script that someone else wrote and you start to see a trained person obediently reading scripts.

Our news casters and pro athletes are more like traveling circus animals than independent thinkers. Most of us working class slouches have more freedom to do and say exactly what we want than our idols on TV do. We shouldn't envy their existences. Their owners have placed a much tighter leash on them regulating what they can and cannot say while out in public. If only more of us had voices in our heads regulating how much we need to eat.

When exactly will Americans start noticing that we've turned into a country of physical train wrecks? Take Donald Trump out of his really expensive suit and put him in a pair of gym shorts and a white tee-shirt, and voila! Walmart shopper! Do you really believe that if there's a God up in heaven that the angels will say, "Well, you've just spent a lifetime being fat, fearful, dumb, and drunk. Welcome to heaven!"? It's a confusing sentence, I know, because our logic really is that retarded.

If there are any higher spiritual beings, isn't it more likely that after you die, having lived a life of being fat, fearful, dumb, and high, that the angels would say, "Dude really? You just like totally slept through the last fifty years of your lifetime and carried out the bidding of sneaky rich people. They used your TV to hypnotize you. We tried thousands of times in thousands of different ways through thousands of different people to wake you from it, but you kept shushing all the divine intervention attempts away. You kept telling people that you got this! So, when would you like to go back?"

It's time to start telling your ego (your addiction's lawyer in your own head) to shut up if you aren't 100% happy with the human being that you see in the mirror each morning. Part of raising your own level of consciousness is re-building a healthy self-esteem. This doesn't involve you being drunk, high, or on confidence (delusion) pills in order to feel good about yourself. Self-respect comes from honorable behavior which involves some hard work and dedication.

Intoxicating ourselves daily isn't going to impress any higher spiritual beings. If they do exist anywhere in the entire universe, then perhaps they're watching and waiting for us to do something good on our own. If you're overweight, then perhaps it's time that you acknowledge that the normal diet has created a herd of self-hating zombie-like people. We'd sooner attack a thin person in our own delusional dialog than get honest with ourselves about our own loss of self-control. We've started defending the insane behaviors that we now share with the growing sub-species of non-paralyzed scooter chair zombies.

It's about damn time that we break the spell and start restoring ourselves into the dignified human beings that we deserve to be. Eight diet cokes a day replaced with eight glasses of distilled water will allow you to drop the extra weight faster than any lies sold on TV. Find other people that also abandoned their own daily sedation. Find healthier people your own age and do what they're doing.

Oppressive and abusive owners want lots of Americans with poor body images and low self-esteems. Functioning addicts will put up with much worse wages and take far more abuse than healthier people with more self-control. Terrible employers need unhealthy people to take their crap (and do nothing to stop it). It's very profitable.

That was the story painted all over the sad city of Cleveland, Ohio. Only a few wealthy sociopaths had hoarded all of the profits and offered a miserable existence to the drunken tattoo-covered working class. Everything had been monopolized. Places like the Mall had only one owner for every five store fronts. The majority of workers there accepted a pathetic existence of poverty that was perpetuated by their own self-medicating addictions. The whole city was a giant prison with no bars.

Most of this book was forged in Cleveland, so I'm not afraid to mention it. Thank God that the people there were unable to turn me into another defeated worker that says, "It is what it is" without attempting to make things better for myself. Ironically Florida has provided a similar social divide paired with an overabundance of sunshine and heat. Thank God for my memories of my middle class existence just north of Atlanta.

If a person hates himself enough, then you can treat him like rubbish and he won't leave because he doesn't have the confidence to do so. Unfair employers depend on masses of cowardly citizens that lack the self-respect to leave bad situations behind them. Certain regions will use and abuse labor more than others. It's up to disgruntled workers to figure things out for themselves.

Right now, a demoralized Clevelander is asking another one, "Whatever happened to Max?" I experienced a revolution in consciousness. Nothing would be more terrifying to our fearless politicians and billionaires than seeing a nationwide boycott on TV watching, alcohol consumption, and prescription drug use. Without those mental shackles our entire world could regain a better quality of living.

The vast labor pool of zombie Americans that have accepted ever-worsening labor conditions could be gone in a matter of months, not years. This is the elites' worst fear, and we could easily make it a reality. Perhaps that's why our borders are being opened up and crazy Muslims are being welcomed in by governments worldwide (like Germany). Oppressive governments and the elites that own them are scrambling to come up with an excuse for troops on the streets. Citizens worldwide are realizing how the world works, and understand that world bankers have been creating debt out of thin air.

Employers have been able to slash wages nationwide with very little pushback from an army of discouraged (not brave), hopeless (not confident), and delusional (full of crap) addicts that

125

think things will magically get better if we just keep doing what we've been doing (insane). The American zombies have been looking for our politicians to make good on any of their promises (insane).

Do you want to be a programmed slave for life? I don't. Stop playing the game the way that our elites have arranged for us to. We're hopelessly hypnotized by a box in our family room that's made them wealthy, and us poor. We must choose to put good fuel into our own operating systems. Then, refuse tomorrow's programming. Stay unplugged from your TV in order to regain full-blown consciousness.

A friend of mine informed me about a book that helped him go from 265 pounds down to a healthy 185 in a matter of six months. The book is called, "The Primal Blueprint" and clearly explains why Americans have gotten so out of shape. When you're not drinking, high, or prescription-pilled into oblivion, do you like the naked person that you see in the mirror? Ask yourself, "Am I the adult that I envisioned growing into when I was a little kid?" If your answer is no, then why not make some changes? Would billionaires distribute a food pyramid that's totally upside down and backward? We all know the answer.

As the public becomes more conscious, it's likely that crooks currently in power will fill the streets with troops. The big problem for world elites (that are throwing Muslim terrorists all over the world via TV) is that consciousness is contagious. People are waking up and beginning to see that it's all part of a long-term scam. If God is watching over this, at some point the angels are going to get pissed. The very diet of poor people is designed to lower their IQs.

Stray away from the normal routine that millions of submissive Americans repeat daily. Once you do, you may actually get different results. It's not a great idea to share the same daily behaviors of moronic people caught on "Jay Walking" that are unable to name the Vice President. Stop going with the crowd, because the crowd has become a little (lot) embarrassing.

There are entire countries that barely drink alcohol or take prescription pills (legalized drugs) at all; their levels of overall happiness are actually higher than ours. The U.S. isn't ranked as the happiest country in the world. We're not even close to the top of the list. We're slipping into a tyranny headed up by control freaks that had bad childhoods and are now dysfunctional adults (with billionaire funding). Our ship is headed for the rocks, so you might want to learn how to swim.

To summarize the nutritional book "The Primal Blueprint" it's all about your body's insulin response to grains, sugars, and high carbohydrate diets. Given that one-third of the public is headed toward type-two diabetes, insulin is relevant. Crazy rednecks and construction workers that drink ten beers a day end up looking like leathery mutants from a post-apocalyptic future. We all see the wrecked bodies of friends and family members that have tried to hide their long-term drinking and drug problems. They're wrecked.

The food pyramid that's been taught to our group is totally upside down. Our bodies will quickly improve if we eat how the hunter/gatherer humans were eating thousands of years ago (before we got office jobs and developed big fat asses that came along with them). Our bodies are genetically programmed to react to the types of foods that we eat each day along with our level of activity.

Nearly everything we've been taught is wrong. Soy protein mimics estrogen, so keep drinking those old-person nutritional drinks and watching Fox News. Man-boobs have become epidemic due to the excess soy protein in American men's diets. American farmers are given huge government subsidies to grow more corn and soy (while not growing other crops). This is a fact. Soy protein also leads to prostate problems. What's the delicious sauce that makes Chinese food go from barely edible to totally awesome? What country has nearly half a billion men that live in total poverty (under Communist rule) and what is it that they're eating all the time?

Don't be easy food for the upper class to feed off of. Ditch the neutered-male diet. I may hang one day just for writing this. In that case, the crime of thought in a dictator's dream will result in a

127

well hung writer. You can eat whatever you want to. As for me, I'm going to look for the wealthiest countries in the world with the highest standards of living and ask, "What do those people eat every day?" If you find that they eat plenty of meat, fat, and there's an absence of an estrogen-mimicking protein (soy) in their diets, then you may want to copy them.

The elites want to keep you hooked on three different expensive prescriptions all of which make you fatter and dumber. Now they're taking poor people's tax returns to pay for the same Obamacare that's used to pay for our daily meds (tranquilizers). It'll soon be weed (Soma). Zanax constantly in your system could add tranquility to some very F'd-up situations. The state wants all citizens to suffer from anxiety, run to your doctors for help, and then get prescribed a lobotomy-in-a-bottle. "If I had a lobotomy in a bottle, the first thing that I'd like to do…" I'm sure you'll be a great Walmart worker in our awesome new global corporation with one global currency. Take your pills, smoke your dope, and stare at a screen on your wall for 5 hours a night (after not working all day).

We've all been trained to eat foods that actually make our bodies store fat rather than burn it for energy. Lots of grains and processed sugars that we've been suckered into eating daily (due to the food pyramid) have caused us to store more fat and burn our existing muscle. Those of us that have always completely disobeyed the food pyramid have ended up being the slender minority. The joke's been on us. Many Americans are starting to look more like "Norm" from the TV show "Cheers" rather than normal human beings. Do you really want to live in an entire country full of male and female "Norms?" What a brave existence to be just another normal American fat guy that drinks or smokes weed constantly and resents his hateful wife.

I witnessed a co-worker drop forty pounds in three months by drinking a gallon of distilled water daily while eliminating all soda. It's all about our body's insulin response to the types of foods that we're eating. Exercise has a whole lot less to do with our weight than we've been trained to believe. Diet soda ruins our health. Fat people love diet soda. If you'd like to stop being overweight then please stop drinking diet soda. Water is the key. Not tap water, but distilled or heavily filtered water.

Start coloring outside of the government-approved guide lines. If you want to get fit and feel good about yourself again, then stop following the food pyramid that was created by our pyramid-scheme government. The guys at the top get rich, and everyone else below them gets used and screwed-over during the process.

Live like a coward and you'll earn the fruits of a coward. A society that allows the sickest and laziest people to live the easiest lives is headed for collapse. "Southpark" has an award-winning episode called, "Raising The Bar" that shows what we've become. Youtube it. If we don't change fast, in about five years you'll start seeing Mexican lawn crews of death cleaning up after the post apocalypse battle. Instead of noisy leaf blowers strapped to their backs, they'll have flame throwers that are used to clean up bloated Americans that were deemed "Not useful" by President Hillary Clinton. Going back to 2014, both Trump and Clinton were included in the earlier editions of this book.

Healthy people won't try to convince you that they're victims of life. They actually tend to believe in the laws of cause and effect and understand the concept of personal accountability. Let's become strong self-sufficient people that can't be oppressed. We must now raise the collective consciousness of the zombie public. If the group thrives, then we get to thrive within it.

Elites (wanting slave-like laborers) need to remember that when you spend a lifetime allowing others to do all of your heavy lifting for you, don't be surprised when your slaves one day realize that they're stronger, faster, and far outnumber the owner-class of society. The general public is allowed to demand rights. Slavery is supposed to be frowned upon by civilized people. Kids get this, but adults worldwide have been failing to do so.

The new "Rise of The Planet of The Apes" movie has little to do with chimpanzees. That movie alone was a huge inspiration for what you're reading. Civilized people have overthrown uncivilized leaders throughout recorded history. Events like the French Revolution have taken place when the ruling class imposed widespread starvation and suffering onto the commoners that served them (today's elites are smart enough to provide food cards and know all about the widely available cheap weed).

It's the former middle-classers that refuse to become $10/hr lifelong drug-addicts that are the largest annoyance to our current elites. Working-class people putting in 50+ hours per week (just to survive) are faster, stronger, and much greater in numbers now than ever before. Poor Americans far outnumber the comfortable reality that's falsely portrayed on TV. Wealthier Americans absolute refusal to raise wages (for the now huge lower-class) has been a greed-fueled miscalculation. The middle class has always provided a buffer zone to defend pampered rich people from rough-ass wage slaves. The buffer zone is gone.

The rich have mistakenly attempted to lock up equally smart middle class people in the same cages with the mega-powerful slave class. Back in the 1970s, people that worked full time could afford houses, cars, and families with the average wage. Not anymore. It's the upper-class that will gladly use violence to maintain their dominance over the rest of the group. The metaphor between servant chimpanzees and lower-class Americans was much less obvious when the Planet Of The Apes movies were first made.

Have you ever observed a wildly unhealthy person giving health advice to a physically and mentally fit person? I know I have. Fat sick people love to dole out health advice. This is like a toothless zombie groaning at a fast smart person that can punch them in the face and run out of the room before the zombie figures out what hit them. At some point, a person's health gets so bad that they lose all touch with reality and begin to view the world through a fun house mirror (provided by their own corrupted ego).

On some level, many Americans have lost their sanity. Was that not also the case in Nazi Germany? What about the completely poverty stricken masses of North Korea? Are they sane people? Are they brave? Are these actual people living in oppressive foreign countries even aware of how bad they have it? If they are aware that they're living in a hellhole, but lack the will to do anything about it, then their own long-term suffering is their fault.

Chapter 11 – Understanding Logic

Think of the human brain as nothing more than a biological computer. By now, most of us have owned multiple computers that operated using the best and worst operating systems available to us at the time. It wasn't that long ago that we had to wait and wait for our computers to simply load the next web page. At some point, most of us have gotten a virus that made our computer stop working correctly. Snoop Dog would call that catching an S T Dizzle! Cheap whores in real life and on the web will throw a wrenches at your processor. Think of this book as an anti-virus program to clean out our brains after years of dealing with our cheap whore politicians and their virus-infected speeches.

We all agree that a computer processes information. We type in a word that we're seeking information about and the computer quickly delivers us the data we've requested. Computers are programmed to perform tasks that solve problems. For instance, the simplest computer that we're familiar with is a calculator, and on it, 2+2=4.

A properly running computer can sort through vast amounts of information quickly and delivers us the answers we're searching for. Has the American public been finding the answers to the problems that our politicians and newscasters have been telling us about for the last ten years? I would argue no; the situation has only grown worse for the majority of people.

Of course all of the retired people collecting Social Security couldn't care less. After all, they're out of the game and set for life (or so they think). American retirees in general watch more TV and as a result are the least conscious of all the types of American zombies. Their brains have been programmed by hours and hours of TV each day. Don't look to them for help, they're gone. Until their government-issued checks (til death) stop coming, they're owned, and will remain obedient. The entire country could literally be burning to the ground and they'd be huddled around their TV sets waiting for the next set of instructions. The retirees living in today's

America are the 100% compliant children-like adults of Orwell's nightmares (and my own).

As a group, we keep asking questions and have failed to get any good answers from the people that we've entrusted to be our protectors. The rest of us just aren't smart enough to run our own lives and that's why we have the government in the first place. If a computer gets a virus, then it stops working correctly.

Sometimes our computers crash completely and don't run at all, but more often than not, our computers slow down. Have the brains of the American people not been slowed-down drastically? Many of us have seen pop-ups about corrupt files on our computers. We also see corrupt politicians popping up on our TVs. Most often, we simply ignore them so long as our computer is still running.

Working-aged adults are now commonly baffled by simple tasks like making change at a cash register. Our population has been mentally handicapped (and handicapped people do require government checks). Low handicap golfers give less capable players free strokes to even-up the match. Healthy American workers are being asked (forced by new laws) to give up more and more strokes (to cheats). The entire burden of providing meals and healthcare to the poor has been loaded on the backs of the healthy (via tax laws) and honest. As always, the wealthy have accounting tricks and tax shelters that allow them to courteously abstain from the process while voting Democrat and telling poor people that they love them (a lot). Honest people become slaves, and cheats win.

The computers in our heads have slowed down drastically due to years of frequent television and drugs. Medicate daily to tolerate the retarded logic on TV and from all of the brainless people that surround us each day. Sedating ourselves daily via constant mind altering drinks and pills has become the only socially acceptable way to cope with living in a dim-witted society.

We're faced with two terrible choices: 1. Be a heartless slave owner that throws crumbs at pathetic poor people below you. Or 2. Be part of the pathetic lower class that accepts deplorable treatment all day long for unlivable wages that nobody respects. Screw both of these choices, because neither is honorable. We must confront shady people, or spend our lifetimes serving them.

Both upper and lower class people are completely blinded by ego and are being pitted against one another by the billionaire architects of our society. Both sides are operating with virus-infected egos. Both groups can get bent because we're bringing back the middle class in America! We're a country that was created by strong, independent, and self-sufficient people. It's in our DNA, and we can teach others how to provide for themselves rather than looking to an all-invasive and all-controlling government for scraps.

Long-term handouts incentivize a victim mentality. Look out, because those who provide meals and housing today will always be demanding something greater in return tomorrow. Human beings always offer free meals and entertainment to someone just before trying to screw them. Dictatorship-style governments have always been accomplished this way.

The fact that the federal government is attempting to control the content of your child's school lunch is a travesty. Only a country of feeble-minded idiots would allow the right to choose your own child's lunch content to be taken away by politicians. Prisoners have no choice in what they eat either. What happened to self-governance and independent decision making? Of course friends of the politicians own the food companies that provide those school lunches (at huge profits).

A clean processor that's virus free is able to easily zip to the next web page. When you ask a virus-free computer what 2+2 equals, it processes the information quickly and accurately just as it was programmed to do. The modern computer is a marvel of engineering that can perform a myriad of complex tasks while storing a ton of old data (memory). What else has a memory, and what do we use our own memories to do? Our memory helps us to make decisions and solve problems based on past experiences. What happens if we can't clearly remember things from our past mistakes?

People with crappy memories become crappy problem solvers. How many Americans have a hard time remembering simple things? We haven't exactly gotten smarter. Ironically, smart phones are creating dumber people by the day. Thanks a lot Steve Jobs! The Patriot Act takes away freedom, the Justice Department protects politicians, and Smart phones destroy intelligence.

We've been robbed of our consciences and good people are suffering as a result. Most of us are hurting others daily without even being aware of it. I don't want my own personal comfort to come at the expense of somebody else's miserable existence. No one else should have a lifetime of poverty imposed on them so that I can live like a king. Back when there was a middle class, moderation was considered reasonable. People were better at sharing. Somehow, control-freak sociopaths have programmed the public to believe that only two extremes now exist. This isn't true.

The human brain is a bio (living)-logical (running on logic) computer that operates using logic and rules that have been programmed into our brains (belief operating systems) throughout our lives. From a young age, **T**raining **V**ideos (TVs) have been conditioning the belief systems of an increasingly stupid group of people. We're trained to believe that if you do this, then that will happen. We watch thousands of repetitive behaviors on TV that are absorbed by our sub-conscious (which then controls 95% of our behaviors). If we spend hours a day watching sociopaths on TV, we then mimic their behaviors. We've unintentionally (and subconsciously) become a country of narcisists.

Our brains are using logic. After being programmed by our parents, teachers and the environment around us, we then come to conclusions based on the existing beliefs in our heads. One child may be taught that if he works very hard at his schooling and gets good grades, then he'll get to go to college. Another child in the same high school may be taught (by his parents) that school's unimportant because that child will be working on the family farm.

Clearly a child's parents can program certain beliefs into their own kids' heads (through repetition). Repetition works. People can easily be programmed to respond to particular situations in totally different ways (depending on who does the programming). As a country, we've unknowingly allowed ourselves to be programmed by sociopaths on a mass level. They've done this

134

using our TVs.

One child is taught by his parents that all Jews are evil and that he must respect the SS guards in the streets. He's then told the same by his teacher (trainer) at school, and gets laughed at and ridiculed by his classmates for simply questioning this belief. The radio newscaster casually makes comments about filthy Jews when the same child turns on his favorite radio show. This child is growing up in Nazi Germany. Entire countries of well-intentioned citizens can be completely trained to believe just about anything. We're no different and have already been subjected to an equally large amount of programming. The elites of earth only struggle with each other regarding who gets to conduct the next ant farm orchestra. When you already have all the money in the world, getting billions of people to build or dismantle things is the one big thrill left.

Through repetition, the general public of an entire country believed Hitler's words (lies) to be the truth. The German masses had been tricked by a small group of corrupt politicians to obtain an evil minority's objective. Would politicians use huge lies via TV (using repetition) to steer the public? History's already answered that question. Germany had suffered greatly after the end of World War One. The German economy had been suffering for over a decade. Their dollars had also lost more and more purchasing power as the years went on. The German public had become very poor, disgruntled, and hopeless. Does any of this sound familiar?

Please don't tell me that you believe that the U.S. economy has improved since 2008. The actual unemployment rate in 2015 is around 20% and nearly 50 million people are on food stamps. 100 million Americans now receive some sort of government entitlement check (Social Security: 40 million, Disability: 10 million, Food Assistance: 50 million). New high paying jobs from emerging industry aren't popping up (unless you're a tattoo-covered 300lb fat guy living in Las Vegas, Nevada). Our current situation in the U.S. is very similar to the conditions prior to the rise of a socialist dictatorship. People are primed and ready to allow somebody else to begin solving their problems.

If people get treated in a degrading manner for a long enough time, eventually they begin to feel like victims. I would argue that the German people had been beaten into a lower level of consciousness that made them more vulnerable targets for Hitler's words (programming). Politicians do attack the psyches of the American masses through speeches on TV. They give us too-good to-be-true promises that involve us investing (complying) in their new control systems and social programs (like Obamacare). If you live in Florida and look at the workforce's missing teeth, dental got left out of the deal.

Rights are lost and demoralized people lack the courage to speak up about shortcomings of billion dollar programs. When they do speak up in opposition to the politicians in power, they're dragged away by private security guards wearing suits and packing guns. We live in a free country everyone. We're super free if we're in total agreement with 4 possible front-running candidates. Don't verbally disagree with any of them in public, or men with guns will politely ask you to leave the discussion.

When economic conditions are terrible for a decade, we become sitting ducks for the next con-man (or woman) that comes along. We begin to seek frequent escapes from reality that end up making us even weaker and more susceptible to getting suckered. We now live in a country that has millions of down-and-out people. Are we beat-down enough yet to accept a full-blown Nanny State?

Logical things that fourth graders can figure out have become baffling problems to many grown adults. Our bodies have an incredible ability to heal when our inner spirit is ignited to do so. If you're down, it's time to get back up. Bravery is being directly injected into your belief system right now. Predators in our world will soon realize that you're one less sheep to feed on.

Having no personal accountability is exactly what the Nazis depended on while they slowly took over and controlled the drunken German public. Nothing here in the U.S. is really any different. Look no further than magic pills and bottles that have reduced our country into a bunch of cowardly lions. This isn't about

136

Americans becoming Nazis; it's about our actions becoming worse and worse without us even being aware of it. We're half sedated all of the time. If you don't think that anti-anxiety pills are keeping people partially sedated all day long, then you're delusional. The ruling elites have successfully neutered working-class men and women.

I've met entire rooms full of spiritual adults that had once done terrible things to their own friends and families while trapped by the insane influence of alcoholism. Many of them quit drinking constantly and became better people. Many didn't. We've all seen people with greater and lesser thresholds of honesty since childhood. No matter what the religious institution or recovery program is, some sad souls will lie until death. That may just be their role in our universe, please don't try to pray away predatory people. They'll always be on the playing field.

America hasn't seen the hope and change that we were all promised back in 2008. That's seven long years ago for the working poor. Time may pass quickly if you're drunk all the time, but it doesn't if you've been working for survival while unmedicated. Being on food stamps for the rest of our lives and working at near minimum wage jobs is a pretty horrific outlook for former middle class people. These types of options yield little fulfillment for previously successful people.

Things haven't turned out very well for our group. I'm betting that most of the German citizens that lived through the Nazi era wish they'd been tipped-off and snapped out of it. They weren't. Call it whatever you want, but there have been times in our lives where we were headed toward certain disaster, but somehow escaped harm. It's called God's grace, and sometimes requires being honest about a bad situation to other people in your immediate life. Many working-class people (that do have resources) are amazingly empathetic when non-addicts that are employed are in their midst. This requires swallowing your pride and laying out your situation to others, AND, WORKING YOUR ASS OFF. Work hard. Eventually, it works.

Rich people love when we keep these things to ourselves. People that worship money above all else much prefer that poor people only pray to an invisible God that never verbally answers. If you do claim to get verbal answers from God, your financially better-off church-going friends will lock your ass up. Spiritually alive people provide help to non-drug addicts while the spiritually dead will recommend for you to go to church (without spending a penny). Actions separate the living from the dead. Aside from my own father, an entire city of the walking dead inspired the birth of this book.

We're not living in Stalin's Russia and the former middle class isn't going to get silently shipped off to Siberia. America is in deep, and no politician on TV from either party is going to dig us out. The true architects of this mess have us digging a ditch just like Cool Hand Luke (only to fill it back in tomorrow). I won't dig my own grave (I'd rather write a very lengthy inscription on it).

We can't repeat mistakes made by whole countries of people that were turned against each other by corrupt politicians using hypnotic speeches. It has happened here in America, but those spells are being broken. We must awaken together without turning on our neighbors like our greedy owners would love to see happen. The politicians don't care about us and their actions (and bank accounts) have made that perfectly clear.

When crooked business owners begin fearing decent employees, (that advocate for themselves) they start hiring less competent people to avoid further employee pushback. Working class Americans can force the greediest owners to dig their own graves. It's our responsibility to apply pressure where needed (and allow nasty business owners to self-destruct). We have to run programs that say hard work and disipline will deliver long-term success.

Chapter 12 – Mental Shackles

After we die, perhaps we'll get an award saying, "Biggest Pushover On Earth" on a nice brass plaque. Imagine a line (outside the gates of heaven) 500 miles long of dejected-looking people carrying around those plaques. When reaching the gatekeeper, the plaque holders are told, "You realize that you perpetuated your own personal suffering, right? Down there, living in fear of terrible people is as close to hell as it gets. All that you had to do to get relief and possibly receive an early release was to act bravely and to speak the truth publically, but you didn't. So, when would you like to go back?"

A person's conscience will tell them that being treated like garbage is wrong, but our consciences can easily be silenced. Can you begin to see the key in front of you? If you're not making enough money to live comfortably, then give yourself a fighting chance by unplugging your cable box. After doing so, you'll more likely be able to out-compete victim Americans. With self-sufficiency comes self-respect. Confidence follows.

Anti-depressants are being over-prescribed. They make people feel confident when there's nothing legitimate to be confident about (just like six beers). Aside from documented chemical imbalances in less than 10% (go back a few decades, when America was healthier) of the general population, the rest of us are totally full of shit (and are just being lazy). If you weren't already diagnosed by your early twenties with a legitimate mental illness, then you're probably just one out of millions of Americans that were completely sold-out by your doctor. What will most people do for money?

Pills that make you feel nothing while your spouse or job are treating you like garbage are no better than drinking or doing illegal drugs daily. They too are shutting off your conscience. Druggies, alcoholics, and prescription pill-poppers make the best victims when it comes to treating somebody like crap and having them do nothing about it. Our logic has been weakened and our owner-class loves the sweet cheap labor that functioning addicts now provide.

If our addiction ever progresses to a non-functioning level don't worry, there are millions of desperate replacements that are ready to fill our spots (while living at home with their parents or roomates). Yes the quality of labor is turning to crap, because employers nationwide have slashed labor rates to maintain their own personal lifestyles (while the U.S. dollar has further depreciated). The workers are all too fearful to make any noise while they slip deeper and more hopelessly into poverty. Once you're down-and-out, you and only you can actually save your self.

Once we're addicted, we lack the capacity to give-a-crap while being abused by others. Leave the giant parade of over-medicated losers that all share two things in common, a government handout and a victim mentality. Nobody feels sorry for them (except for themselves). TV, weed, pills, and drinks clearly haven't solved their major life problems. Try removing known hypnosis (TV) paired with neurotoxins (weed or alcohol) and see what happens to your luck. Health creates wealth. Work hard.

If I'm a greedy billionaire, (World Bankers, CEOs, Board Members, and crooked politicians) then I'd want as many of those pill-poppers and TV watchers as possible. Those in the business of screwing people over for money love doing business with a country of marks. Labor rates are the lowest since the Great Depression, and a country of addicts is too brain-dead to adjust for inflation. 40 hour work week, nah, let's make it 60. I never could have imagined back in 2005 that workers just 10 years later would surrender 20 additional hours per week for the same amount of purchasing power.

Billionaires don't want you so incapacitated that you don't show up for work anymore, but just enough so they can treat you like crap. Employers want to keep Americans right on the edge without us quitting or having the guts to confront them. Any former employer of mine knows that when they acted shady and decided to piss on my feet, then I've called them out on it.

If bosses act shamefully, then speak the truth regarding their shameful behavior and let them feel uncomfortable. This has happened in my life during the creation of this book and has only resulted in more pleasant jobs with higher wages. My own working conditions improved because I brought my bosses' unsavory business practices into the light. If people are acting shamefully to maintain their comfort, become an accurate mirror for them. Vampires can't see themselves in mirrors and must avoid sunlight (truth).

The cold-blooded ownership class of America is only playing dumb regarding solution pills and alcohol that are constantly advertised on TV. Elites absolutely want a country of functioning pill-poppers and pot-heads because they'll do the most work for the lowest wages possible. I suppose billionaires may be doing the same with the low-level politicians that serve them.

We all know how human beings respond when authority figures tell us not to do something. Back in the 80's, our politicians on TV came up with the ultimate con for Americans, "Just say no." U.S. prisons had just been privatized and set up for profit. Politicians suddenly had the ability to become share holders for privately owned prisons and wouldn't you know it, those prisons got filled up to capacity. The war on drugs was launched at exactly the right time to fill up those newly privatized (for profit) jails. Look this up. It was all a calculated for-profit plan that's tied in with government subsidies (a racket).

People tell us not to do something, then, we do more of it! Billionaires figured this out a long time ago and have been using reverse psychology on the public for thousands of years. Is it possible that our billionaires have out-smarted the zero-dollar-aires now watching ape training videos for hours a night? We're literally watching repetitive Training Videos that show us where to pawn away all of our stuff. When food, rent, electricity, and car payments are on the line, it's no coincidence that asset liquidation stations have exploded across the country since 2008.

A country full of addicts is very easy to fleece. If I just gained 100 extra pounds, covered myself in tattoos, and started wearing all black every day, then I'm pretty sure that a line of defeated Americans would start forming in front of me. Then I could simply pile up their stuff and then sell it back to them later for a huge profit. Have you ever wondered why the poorest Americans that are on food stamps are still able to afford the largest flat screen TVs? Is it possible that billionaires wanting slave-like labor have replaced physical chains with televised programming?

Americans are constantly drinking alcohol and taking drugs (prescription or illegal) that reduce their brain function down to a level too low to legally drive. Think about people that you've personally known that were close to mentally retarded, and still received their driver's license. The bar isn't exactly high. Think about senior citizens that can't remember what they ate for breakfast, are unable to work a DVD player, and can't promptly remember their own kids' names, and still, they too are able to drive legally. An out-of-it senior citizen and a drunk driver operate motor vehicles in a very similar manner. Both parties are suffering from impaired judgment and a lack of motor skills. The brains of senior citizens that have trouble driving cars are operating at a diminished capacity.

Do you really want to share the same amount of brain power as a racist 85 year-old man that can't drive a car in a straight line? This is perhaps the least reasonable segment of our population. All of which, receive a government check and watch Fox news all day while eating like horses.

Sure 21-year-olds with young fresh brains can drink often for a few years, but older people with older bodies can't. It makes them nearly retarded along with all of their blood-thinning meds. Old people in America are now proud of reading the newspaper, going to the store, and producing a bowel movement. Congrats, and thank you for not tipping well.

Retired Americans are also the people that show up and vote (legitimizing a completely illegitimate governing system that gives them monthly checks). Welfare recipients and old people are the most loyal voters in America. Working Americans aren't given the day off to vote (even though their tax dollars pay for everything).

We've established that moronic people can still legally drive cars. Yet, alcohol and some prescription pills are reducing our abilities below that level. If you're doing this to yourself multiple days a week, or worse, every day, then what do you think it's doing to your overall problem solving abilities? Criminals remain in charge, and we accept whatever the next round of bad news is. We'll always wake up in bed the next morning, reach for coffee, and then return to our horrible jobs for our next round of beatings. What magnificent creations of God we've become. How proud the angels above must be.

Stay poor, and stay down. Owning cars and not receiving public assistance is simply an upper-class privilege. It's all been designed so that we lack the time, energy, or self-respect to escape our plight. We readily accept the television programming that they've carefully prepared for us (to advance their own selfish agendas). The TV is used to program the human that's sitting in front of it. Please YouTube "TV is mind control."

The flicker rate of our television is about 30 frames per second. The human brain can only last a few minutes at that rate of stimulation before your critical thinking ability is turned off. You then become a trainable ape that dresses itself, can talk, and does chores for the slightly smarter owner-class of America all day long. We continue absorbing news content without questioning its validity.

Just picture a space ship that has a force field shielding it from space debris. Then, picture your brain having the same type of force field that shields you from bullshit presented by politicians that have been caught lying to you hundreds of times before. That natural force field is shut off within minutes of sitting in front of your TV. The alpha waves in your brain transition into a more suggestive state.

Would power crazy billionaires take advantage of that kind of power? Even the best of souls are defenseless when subjected to just minutes of television. We're watching other people on TV lie, cheat, and steal for money all day long. We're watching a bombardment of images of others doing heartless things in order to drive a nicer car and have sex with better looking sexual partners. Is this the meaning of life?

Admitting that you've been conned is a lot easier when someone else admits it first. These poor souls have failing health, and due to their meds (drug habit), many of them are unable to achieve an orgasm. Our bodies are our true vehicles for experiencing life, not our shiny cars. You are not your car.

Orwell wasn't bullshitting us when he wrote about the government one day setting out to abolish the orgasm. All of you that got conned into taking some form of Prozac know exactly how close to home this statement is. Watch "Equilibrium" to see what's being taken away from us. Feeling nothing at all is much worse than experiencing the non-medicated ups and downs of being alive.

Very few of us are so dangerous without meds that we must be tranquilized by our government-subsidized sellout doctors. All of which, drive nicer cars and likely have bigger houses than you do. If you're a dangerous person when you stop taking your meds, then please keep taking them. Most Americans weren't born mentally ill. Doctor's patients all get fatter and sicker while a bunch of pharmaceutical-grade witch doctors sling pills at everything. Which pills are right for you, and which pills will keep that doctor in his brand new Benz?

Our group can change real life outcomes by simply holding rich criminals accountable. How many bankers got locked up after they lied, cheated and stole from the American people in 2008? I don't accept sociopathic behaviors in front of me without letting the person know (in a very polite way) that they're behaving ridiculously. If someone wants me to help them, then they have to behave appropriately. Due to my own lack of fear, their bad behaviors go away and I'm left with a more reasonable environment to work in. That's why people from around the world immigrated to America. Brave citizens spoke up and kept assholes in check.

The working class in America must realize that if we stand our ground with sociopaths, then we'll begin to raise our own quality of living. There are more of us, and if we call them out in a group effort, then they'll nearly always back down when confronted with the ugly facts. Don't be afraid to do what's right. Our lives will begin to get better again when we start showing some guts.

We did watch the entire banking and mortgage industry nearly collapse in 2008 due to blatant in-your-face fraud. Then, to any critically thinking person's astonishment, zero punishment came. These mortgage and derivative scams decimated the net worth of millions of good Americans. By all means, they are replaceable. The world wouldn't blink if all banking criminals and politicians were fired and stripped of their power tomorrow. There'd more likely be a thunderous applause. The public's loyalty to the ruling elite runs no deeper than any cat's or dog's to the person that feeds it. If the dog class of citizens passes 50%, then you'll find yourself in a dictatorship.

We might as well call them out and take away from them what they've already taken away from too many of us. Emails existed between shady bankers. The gigantic NSA facility in Utah likely still has all of it. You know, the data storage facility that stores everything that we've ever done on the internet (since 911).

Many of us had families that were broken apart while our assets vanished. Bankers that made those decisions ought to experience the same loss of financial comfort. Police, military, and riot control, why on earth are you defending the bankers? There were paper trails, emails, and phone conversations; all of which would provide more than enough evidence to prosecute hundreds of banking criminals. Nothing has been done to that effect.

The court of public opinion still exists, but is being silenced by desperate politicians creating Net Neutrality legislation. If politicians give something the label of neutral, then the public ought to know that there's nothing neutral about it. In "1984" Big Brother would install a bunch of internet regulators that are in charge of internet censorship and call them Hate Speech Protectors. Crush all dissent.

Only by delivering the message via TV could such a massive scam like the 2008 Bank Bailout be pulled off. The Bankers clean out our life savings, jobs are lost by the millions, and we do nothing. What a bunch of cowards we are. That, or our TVs have had us walking around under the control of somebody else for a very long time.

The American people did nothing, aside from watching a tiny fraction (of a percentage point) of our population protest on TV and promptly get pepper-sprayed in the face by trained morons for the criminal act of telling the truth. Television has trained a couple hundred million people to believe that, if you're an average American speaking the truth and asking for justice against criminal bankers, then you'll get pepper-sprayed in the face. We were all trained to stay home and stay quiet. It worked. If the ruling class wasn't desperately attempting to maintain control, then they wouldn't be broadcasting terror attacks around the world.

Do you get that billionaires get to choose what news images get burned into our brains? Do you get that watching protestors get brutalized and arrested will modify the behavior of the group to stay home and keep your mouths shut? It worked on me. This is mind control 101. It's very simple logic that anyone can understand. Computers can easily be programmed, and so can we.

Chapter 13 – Muzzled And Caged American Superheroes

The public is all wrapped up watching "reality" TV and professional sports (all while drinking and smoking ourselves into oblivion). When was the last time that we saw a professional athlete speaking out against political corruption? Weird how all of our real life super heroes seem to be completely satisfied with our government, the politicians, and the entire 911 lie. Professional athletes aren't exactly opening up small businesses to employ their fans that can no longer afford tickets at the stadium.

Our pro athletes are nothing more than the caged (totally separated from the public) performers that we see featured in the Russell Crowe movie, "Gladiator." I'd argue that pro athletes enjoy much less freedom than an average American does. How so? The amount of time practicing, training, traveling, and performing that pro athletes are obligated (forced) to do in order to get paid by their owners greatly limits their amount of time free. Each one of their mansions is like the polar bear exhibit at the zoo.

Then, their owners give them the ridiculously Orwellian title of, free agents. There's nothing really free about their existence. I have much more free time than they do, and I don't want the deal that they've negotiated for themselves. In this pivotal time in American history pro athletes currently mean zero in the equation. In reality, pro athletes are the world's most distracting pawns. One on one, pro athletes could beat most of us to death. However, well-crafted speeches that are delivered by a slender man in a suit on our TV (the President) have slain the public opinion of 150 million people (with a declining quality of life). Speeches direct armies, not muscle.

Why is it that we put pro athletes on such a pedestal? Docs an average Joe not have the ability to eat as much food, have as much sex, and have a roof over his head? The only difference being that the average Joe actually has a lot more free time. Even people on food stamps and disability checks get food, sex, and shelter. The general public enjoys much more free speech than pro athletes do. Our pro athletes are more like traveling circus animals that have lost the gift of speech.

Did it ever occur to the public that very wealthy men may want to separate the fastest, strongest, and most disciplined humans from the rest of us? Working alongside pro-athletes would encourage the average Joe. We all get a lot braver when we're working alongside other strong, fast, and brave people. Confidence is contagious, and abusive business owners hate that.

Have you ever seen a smaller person run their mouth while out with one of their very large friends? The genetically strongest warriors have been separated from the general workforce. A whole factory full of mediocre workers will keep their mouths shut for a lifetime. Wages stay low, and workers stay quiet.

The reason that pro athletes haven't been speaking out against corrupt bankers (that purposely crashed the US economy into the ground in 2008) is because they too have owners that would ban them from the league. Our athletes fear losing their money (their true God) for speaking out on behalf of the public. Stop watching paid-off people that don't care about us.

Do you remember Maximus from the movie "Gladiator" turning the crowd against the Emperor? Do you get that even our millionaire pro athletes have been silenced and politically neutered by their billionaire team owners? Sounds like athlete Speech Neutrality rules have already been put into place by the owners. If that wasn't the case, then somebody would be speaking out on behalf of the fifty million Americans on food stamps, but they don't.

Pro athletes could wield a great deal of influence over the masses to bring about positive societal change if they weren't terrified of losing their money. They're more trained to keep their mouths shut than the rest of us are, because TV cameras are on them. Their actions on camera can change public opinion, so, they're forbidden to do and say as they please.

The public worships pro athletes and actors like Gods. In return, not one multi-millionaire pro athlete walks away from their owners and fights on behalf of the fans. I challenge any famous pro athlete (that supposedly believes in God) to start fighting for the true best interests of the American public. It's a total joke that our strongest, fastest, and most determined Americans all have owners that won't let them speak. Instead, blatantly obvious corruption by bankers and politicians goes completely uncontested by our idols. When it comes down to helping millions of suffering Americans, our pro athletes do nothing but distract us.

We all know the truth, but none of us want to face it. Otherwise we might have to improve ourselves instead of vicariously living our dreams through some other guy on TV (that doesn't give a crap about us). If even a single one of our pro athletes stuck their own neck out on behalf of the American people to prevent a second great depression, it could cause the tides to turn for the better. If the sports fans really wanted to get their heroes' attention, then perhaps an empty stadium on game day would do it. The fans have power too, lots actually.

Our pro athletes have been rewarded (bribed) millions of dollars for their hard work (servitude), dedication (obligation), and their God-given gifts (steroid use). If this book ever makes it into the hands of a pro athlete that has always praised God, then I ask, "How bad do things have to get for the millions and millions of fans that have worshipped you as their hero before you speak out?" Please grow a conscience and start fighting for the rights of God fearing people. If one of today's pro athletes chose to do so, they could earn a place in world history alongside Martin Luther King Jr. That trumps all current athletic accomplishments. Trump Trump by speaking out.

The absolute silence of our pro athletes will surely be rewarded with silence regarding their existences in history books. Sports records will become completely irrelevant if the United States falls apart like the former Soviet Union already has. One of the more disturbing things about professional sports and their power to distract the masses is that Hitler outlined how pro sports would be used to do just that, distract us all. Huge stadiums were a German design. To truly learn from our past, we must examine our history.

The History channel has recently shown lengthy documentaries about Hitler's takeover of the minds of the German masses in an effort to prevent history from repeating itself. That's History channel 2. The primary History channel has been reduced to reality TV featuring: Pawn Stars, Counting Cars, American Pickers, and Swamp People. Surely watching those shows (while getting high) will educate us all regarding world history. There's no music on MTV and no history on the History Channel.

Our strongest, fastest, and most fierce competitors have been paid-off to stand aside while corporate dictators shipped millions of American jobs overseas. This caused millions of Americans to lose everything while the top 1% has grown wealthier. This is a fact. Politicians then carefully pacify the public with words via the next televised speech.

If there's ever been a time in recent history that divine intervention was needed, this is it. There's divinity within all of us. Deep inside of every person is a voice of right and wrong. Many of us, including our pro athletes have had that conscience silenced. Doing the right thing and telling the truth may not prevent bad things from happening to us, but that doesn't mean we should stop. Maybe it's meant to be that our souls get really lost in the dark in order for us to crave the light once again. We all have great potential to do some good while here. Let's stop watching others be great (at trivial pursuits). We can become brave people that our pro athletes are impressed by.

Chapter 14 – Consciousness Conquers Fear-Based Beliefs

Take a second to stop and imagine that this whole thing that we call life is just a game that our souls volunteered for before birth. Then, in order for all of our souls to learn as much as possible on a spiritual level, we also agreed to forget who and what we really all are; a conscious being having a human experience. After we're dead, this will all seem a lot less important.

The veil of forgetfulness will allow our souls to embark on "dangerous" missions in the darkest of places in order to test our bravery or lack thereof. If everybody knew beyond the shadow of a doubt that we all have indestructible souls, then this ride wouldn't be that exciting. Have you ever worked at a family owned business? Were the children of the owners more or less worried about getting fired for slacking off than the non-family members? Less, right? Human nature is to get away with what we can. Therefore, if we knew for sure that we have immortal souls that will continue on after death, then we wouldn't take this game so seriously.

Do you think tyrants want you believing that you have an immortal soul on a learning experience? I don't. Tyrants prefer that we believe in a one-shot Godless human lifetime that will cease entirely when we die. They want us to believe in a random accident of intelligent life that only occurred here on planet earth (in the entire universe). That way, we remain controllable when guns are pointed at us. A tyrant's greatest weapon against vast numbers of people (that could easily overpower them) is a lack of spirituality. This results in an intense fear of death that serves tyranny well.

If billions of people worldwide are suffering while running on fear-based belief systems, then I'm creating a program that crashes them. If the program truly works, then tyrants (which we all agree are bad) will be overrun by awakened citizens worldwide. Instead of chaos resulting as the tyrants would like us to believe, we can create a less hostile world to live in. The group creates the world that we're living in. Let's take the paint brush out of the tyrant's hand.

People lacking a belief in an afterlife (or worse, the trained belief that they're going to hell when they die) greatly fear death. Organized religion (crime) has been used to condition the public to live lifetimes of fear. The ruling class (that follows none of the rules) then gets richer in the process while the ignorant public pays them taxes for protection. It really is a great scam.

All well-off church employees that take money from poor people while failing to provide practical job training, education, and 7 day per week food and shelter (given that there's a building that was constructed using church donations) ought to be banned from attending church. That, and they should shoot themselves in the heads for using God as a money making scheme. Too much? Have you ever stopped and considered that churches are the perfect tax-free vehichle for money-laundering? Maybe the public are a bunch of rubes.

Ok zombies, here's a hint. Remember the TV series Ozark on Netflix? It was a great series. When illegal businesses generate lots of cash that people want to avoid taxes on, they make deals with other businesses that take in cash. Then, any governing officials that are supposed to be catching said crimes are given a cut of the profits to avoid having crappy lives that their actual wages would afford. Officials then miraculously have beautiful cars along with houses and families in spite of being less-than-impressive people. In the end, nobody get's busted, money continues to get cleaned, and the people involved in the racket think that God's ok with all of it (so long as they're constantly recommending church to everyone). Oh Max, we're just blessed! Uh huh, that's it, I'm sure.

If you've known people for years and years that always seemed to have tiny consciences and then became massively religious while also piling up houses, cars, motor homes, and you name it, then their enthusiasm for organized religion may be related to their love of money. Churches and charities are (and have been) used to launder cash and zombies need to figure this out. A world where only the crooks are winning is some major bullshit. When scammers take over everything, good people will experience hellish lives while acting honorably. Some regions are hellholes and are best to walk away from.

Ever heard of the Vatican? Don't be alarmed, that tingling sensation in your head is a thought. Does it now make sense why the most money-worshipping married couples you've ever known (that give cheapskates a bad name) have such boners for organized religion? Have priests and preachers already been caught in other scandals? So they have been caught molesting children and embezzling church funds, but laundering money using accounting tricks is beyond the limits of greed? Has the connection between Italian mobsters attending Catholic church eluded you?

If you've constructed a church building using donations from less fortunate church members, and don't use that same building to house them after they've lost their jobs and homes, then please remove yourself from this game. Churches are supposed to be like long term insurance policies for when the shit hits the fan in real life. If you live long enough, in some way or another, it happens. People do lose jobs, houses, and spouses.

If the church isn't there to help put back together destroyed people, then what's it there for? The vast majority of churches stay locked up and empty for the majority of the time (like rich peoples' vacation homes in Florida). Didn't Jesus Christ frequently cuss-out the church people of his time for their hypocrisy?

Strong evidence of advanced beings has been put into writing by ancient cultures and has been disregarded and discredited by our kings and their priests for thousands of years. Kings have sold humanity the most convenient version of reality in order to rule over us all. If a historical event can undermine a king's authority, then they make it disappear from the historical record.

People from the distant past were full-blown morons, and still we continue being dominated by the same smoke and mirrors that worked on Ancient Idiots (future History channel show about us). I can't wait to grow-out my hair super long and become a commentator. Carlin did it. Watch his first on-air appearance on TV, it's on youtube. Clean cut, well spoken, and parents in the business. By 40, the overwhelming BS of the world and being lied to by money-worshipping people was enough for him to begin ranting. Being conscious and calling out liars is an honest trade.

This is our opportunity to be thankful for everything that we've learned and change strategy. Please don't cuss-out God for letting us explore in the universe without constant help. This is the same freewill that we all want so badly. We all want to do what we want without others telling us what we can or cannot do. Our TVs and smart phones have been used to steal it from us, and it's being returned right now.

America stood for freedom, liberty, and independence. Most of you remember the phrase, "Taxation without representation." I'd argue that both organized religion and the federal government have done the same thing to a bunch of TV-brainwashed talking monkeys. The elite collect taxes from an increasingly poor citizenry and then use those same tax dollars to build mansions, fly around the world in private jets, and eat $100 meals each day.

Have you ever seen a small toddler swat away their parent for trying to help them to do something new? When the toddler predictably gets hurt after trying the new activity on their own, they then turn around and cuss-out their parent (for allowing them to get hurt). This is exactly the same behavior of the average suffering American. We can't have it both ways. People across the country seem to be angry with God when it's the political elites that have been feeding off of us all like vampires. Their food is beginning to turn on them. It's been a stunning site to see.

We need to help ourselves with the freewill that God allows us to have. We all need to stand up to the bullies in our lives. If we demonstrate bravery, then we at least stand a chance for a less hostile world to live in. These are lessons that were learned during grade school. Let's not behave like infantile adults that are incapable of providing for ourselves. If we want others to provide everything, then they'll own us. Greedy people holding vast resources love vast groups of impoverished people that will do their bidding. When local slaves become too disobedient, open up the borders to allow a replacement hoard to attack and replace us.

Politicians have literally been waging war against their own tax-bases.

A 90 year-old man in Florida was arrested for feeding the homeless in 2014. It's a crime to feed the homeless? National (tax exempt) charities and government officials don't want local citizens cutting out the middle man. Citizens helping citizens is the key to solving all of this. All of us need to start creating solutions for poor people so they lose dependence on tax-funded programs.

During this planned worldwide economic collapse, governments want to remain the go-to food source for hopeless people. Zombie church people are much more likely to recommend that you pawn away all of your belongings than sacrifice a single meal to help a stranger. Their bulging waistlines and brand new cars prove this point. Politicians and church officials worship money and their own personal comfort (not God). Otherwise, they'd start becoming less comfortable while helping down-and-out people to get back on their feet again. The public acts like dogs under the dinner tables of the ownership class.

If our current economic system keeps getting worse, then an already prepared replacement system that offers more food and handouts (but is totally worse for the majority of hardworking people) will soon be rolled out. Poor people that do need food assistance will embrace the new system with open arms. This is why the 90 year-old Florida man was arrested for feeding the homeless. This all has to do with world bankers that are attempting to consolidate power and finalize a one-world currency that they will control. Instead of a utopia, it becomes a slave-like labor system enforced by a global army. Only when we become aware of a predator that's headed in our direction can we turn toward it and defend ourselves.

Please shatter your delusions that church preachers and politicians are going to help save you, they're not. Their bank accounts, houses, and cars reveal their motives. Unplug your TV and start saving yourself now. We can't have it both ways if we want to learn new activities on our own. If earth is a training ground for young souls (and a school that we'll eventually graduate from) then perhaps it's time that we start standing up to the school bullies both here and now. Perhaps the lesson to be learned is that if you don't stand up to a bully, then you deserve to be bullied. The bully is simply doing his (or her) job. Forcing confrontations with assholes (he's, she's, or not-sure's) can prevent years of pathetic servitude to them.

If you see others that are weaker than yourself being harmed, then have a conscience and stand up for them. Turning a blind eye to save your own ass is a cowardly way to exist. Only men and women without consciences sit by silently while the weak and the innocent get bullied by wicked people. A world in which it's every man for himself is a world that's constantly at war (just as Orwell's 1984 described). Orwell, (a former government worker in real life) made it clear that those in charge of socialist systems enjoyed dominance, not charity.

It only makes sense that when you find yourself lost in a very dark place (and can't see a positive thing) to seek light. When you find that light, you then become enlightened. This is the journey from a low level of consciousness (where you feel powerless) to an enlightened level of consciousness (where you're at peace with God). At that point, you cannot be bought, sold, or manipulated into doing the bidding of wicked people. You will be free.

Most people wear their guilt more loudly than they could ever imagine. Guilty souls walking around on earth are about as obvious to conscious people as a 250lb bearded-man dressed up in a My Little Princess outfit for Halloween. Nobody's buying the façade. The truthful and liars among us shine through to the conscious. Unconfident people gang-up together and hurl insults at the living.

A corrupted political system would invest a lot of money to steer the masses away from a high consciousness diet while loading the system itself up with tons of guilty consciences. Government is often a criminal gang. Tyrants can't rule over large groups of highly enlightened people. Too many people will sacrifice themselves to protect the God-given rights of others. Americans are about to show the world whether or not we still have any bravery in our genes.

Seeing is believing. How many times have we all heard that expression? This is where the elites that see the American people as little more than a large herd of well-trained zombies have got us by the brains. Television (Tell...A...Vision) shows us exactly who is in charge, while telling us what to think about it. The people that control what's shown on TV then control what we believe in. They choose all predictable human reactions, only if, you watch their programming.

If you own the media companies and have billions to spend, then the public sees exactly what you want them to. The public is seeing and believing exactly what the owners want us to. Refuse the programming. We all can choose to not watch TV. Then, billionaires lose their ability to control our thoughts, beliefs, and opinions.

Which person is more likely to worship money over all else, the common man or the billionaire? Since the advent of TV, the masses have been programmed by those who worship money. The moral values of America have gotten worse as the amount of television that we watch has increased. As a group, we've been set up for failure by an invention that has allowed dictators and tyrants to tell us their visions.

In February of 2015, our political elites revealed new laws that are called "Net Neutrality." The public has the right to reject censorship of free speech and call for the resignation of all public officials supporting losses of freedom. They work for us. We won't put up with tyrannical leaders because to do so would be un-American. If we lose free speech, then we're complying to tyranny.

Billionaires and the governments that they control are now censoring the internet. The masses aren't all brain-dead zombies. We can see why the sharing of information online is now being controlled. Facebook and YouTube videos absent of profanity and vulgarity are now frequently being censored. Truth can't be restrained forever when billions of people are involved in the game.

I've personally had non-profane videos deleted from my Facebook timeline as if they never existed. Many Youtubers have also been blowing the whistle. I was always under the impression that Americans valued freedom of speech. Politicians that are financially backed by billionaires are free to make speeches, but we're not? How was it that Abraham Lincoln fought for our freedoms? If there's truth in our words, they'll resonate. Wicked people are horrified by free speech. So speak freely already, it's like sunlight to vampires.

The other recent revelation on television is that everything that we do on the internet is now being monitored by the NSA (for our safety of course). Let's make everything electronic because there's no way that someone can cause chaos in your life if the power goes down or someone hacks into our account. The American people should be out in the streets and at politician's front doors over this issue, but we're not. The actual level of ongoing internet censorship isn't being televised. The closest thing to the truth that we get from TV these days comes from comedians. They've become our modern day philosophers telling us truths about our own reality that are so absurd that we must laugh rather than cry. A lengthy pianist named Owen Benjamin knows all about censorship.

Throughout history there have been philosophers that have attempted to define the meaning of life. These men and women have shared the common goal of seeking truth and obtaining knowledge. An enlightened person sees deeper into situations. An ignorant person reacts without thinking on a daily, monthly, and lifetime basis. They're victims of life. Ignorant people become pawns for the men and woman that control the chessboard via cash. Perhaps comedians have become our last line of defense in their attempts to reason with us. They use comedy and logic to speak truths about the insane world that we have to live in, but don't particularly care for. We can make things better, but must confront crooks. There's lots of them out there, and it'll take crowds of non-crooks to take them down. This is why we must awaken the zombies. Until they work for us, they'll be serving the crooks. Does that make sense?

Words wield more power than any physical confrontation is capable of. Broadcast a message and millions of people can be liberated, or imprisoned by it. Dictators use words (and images) to take away personal power. They dictate the direction that you'll go. Liberators use speech to unlock the power within all of us. Their words break the bonds that hold people in servitude to thieves. Fear can be melted away with knowledge, and mental walls vanish.

Many of us have been forced to do things that we know aren't right in the name of money. We've been asked to do these things by wealthier men that are holding food and shelter over our heads. If we don't comply with cruel orders, then we eventually lose our jobs and our families. In poor economies, this is a reality. We've been managed (man…aged) by fear, not love. Money has replaced God, and science has turned into conmen's-science. The best way to pull off a huge con is by using false science. Just ask Nasa. Since the creation of this book, their own credibility has crumbled under internet scrutiny.

The wealthy have offered most of us (the current working-aged public) deals that say: if we're willing to hurt other working-class people, then the wealthy business owner will pay us enough money to afford adequate food, shelter, and entertainment to attract a decent companion. We're constantly told to accept degrading treatment in exchange for enough money to live (survive). Those people with the highest levels of consciousness end up with two terrible choices in a corrupted area:

1. Lower your own consciousness with alcohol and drugs to "play ball" with the slave owners.

2. Refuse to compromise your values and suffer the consequences for being ethical in an area that's now run by assholes.

The public determines how long abusive employers are going to stay in business. We've forgotten this. Our TV-hypnotized women aren't reinforcing good behaviors of American men either. Just like in ancient Rome right before the fall of that empire, many women have been reduced to trading sex for financial stability (in order to avoid this brutal job market). American women are just as guilty as the men for the sad state of affairs. Remove yourself from the zombie diet and you'll cease to remain a whip master living in a demoralized city.

The laws of cause and effect still apply to all of us. People like "The Situation" become millionaires, and Michael Hastings and Edward Snowden are considered enemies of the state. If evil men dominate a particular area, then we're not supposed to be striving to become the most comfortable Nazis living in Hitler's Germany. Life in America became less and less comfortable for honorable people between 2000 and 2016. As economies slide downward, so do morals. We must harness our frustration and use it to create something positive.

How are higher spiritual beings supposed to respect us if we don't even respect ourselves? If we want God to step in and give humanity some divine intervention, then perhaps we ought to start by doing some brave deeds first. Try showing God that we actually believe in a spiritual hierarchy of which billionaires aren't at the top. They're not.

Letting our spouses hurt others all day while plugging our ears and closing our eyes isn't going to get us into heaven. My best guess is that we'll be asked to repeat life again until we act with some dignity. Prescription pills and alcohol make lying to ourselves about our shady partner's actions much easier. Refuse to watch TV and you'll begin to regain your natural conscience. If humanity is the most spiritually gifted group of beings in the entire universe, then would somebody please shoot me in the head. Fear of getting whacked by tyrannical leaders shouldn't govern the actions of free men. If you can't speak freely, then you're not free. Does that make sense?

Good parents don't reward (reinforce) the bad behaviors of their children. Why would God be any different? Having a screen in our homes that's been proven to alter our brain waves (placing the viewer in a suggestive state) is a quick way to catch a virus that will slow down the processor in your own head. This only makes the existing problems in your own life seem more unsolvable. None of the quick easy fixes actually work. Hard work and consistent effort deliver results.

TV has been taken over by corporate interests. A high ranking national defense official on Stephen Colbert recently stated that he hasn't watched TV for the last 20 years because, "It turns your brains into cotton candy." Mr. Colbert then sarcastically defended TV. The government official then recommended that the audience read a book instead. My best guess is that any House or Senate member that would publically propose that TV is mind control would be found floating in a river somewhere. Perhaps it's time to "Kill Your TV" as a popular YouTube video recommends.

Tons of corporate zombies require prescription anti-depressants (not you of course) just to keep showing up for their weekly soul draining. Has it ever occurred to them that maybe they're depressed because they've been acting like dogs? If you've read this far without suffering an aneurism, then this may be the turning point where things in your life start to get better. If you did suffer an aneurism, then congratulations, you're dead!

If your life is already really good, but you know somebody else that has nothing left to lose, then perhaps this book can snap them out of it. It's helped others already. People with nothing left to lose are often the most teachable because their ego's taken such a beating. Only when we have nothing left of value, do we become willing to try a new strategy.

Chapter 15 – How To Unplug Yourself From The Matrix

The struggle between a verbally spoken set of values from a measly one hour per week church service vs. four hours per day of televised sex is over. When it comes to forming beliefs, it's like a butter knife vs. a machine gun. If you're a preacher that wants to vastly improve the spirituality of your congregation, then have them try unplugging their TVs for an entire month. The television has slaughtered all organized religions. Television is teaching the public their current belief systems because seeing, is believing.

What's the other statement that we often say about something that we're verbally told but can't see? Talk is cheap. Our brains have been conditioned not to believe what someone tells us without showing us the proof. TV is therefore the greatest device ever created when in the hands of a liar that can afford all of the TV time in the world. Human beings do own the TV networks, right? Are they rich people or poor ones? Which group of people tends to play fair and operate using more ethics? Marketing teams with multi-million dollar advertising budgets can (and do) sell the public whatever they want to.

Church has become a brief masturbatory behavior. Can you imagine Jesus Christ, Buddha, Mohammed, or Moses performing small miracles in front of people for one hour per week, only to have the people go home to a 50 Inch flat screen? The television easily bulldozes over all spiritual teachings in a matter of minutes.

Perhaps Christ's second coming will be him flying around the whole world in one night. He'll visit everyone's house just like Santa, smashing all of their TVs with a sledge hammer. A few weeks later, (after discovering that all of the TVs on earth had been smashed to dust along with their factories) billions of pale bloated zombies would slowly begin to regain consciousness. Smart phones would be gone too. We all did so much better when home phones were it. Can we vote to go back to that?

When the Macintosh computer first came out, there was a TV commercial of a "1984" future with a hero hurling a hammer at a giant TV screen. Steve Jobs saw what his inventions would eventually do for humanity (render TV, obsolete). It's as if that giant hammer thrown back in 1984 has been traveling in slow motion for the past 31 years. It may have taken my lifetime to reach the screen, but it's the blink of an eye in human history.

The one-way communication device that only favored the super wealthy now has a two-way replacement. Computers with internet access are to TV, what automobiles were to the horse and carriage. The public got access to the tree of knowledge and took a big damn bite before censorship algorithms were put in place. Giant secrets making the elites look like assholes have already leaked worldwide.

You've heard of cars with a governor on them so that they can't go past a certain speed, right? How would you like to remove the governor that's been wrecking your ability to learn new things and retain valid information? The formula for unrestricting your own brainpower is being delivered right now.

I'm not programmed for hours a day because I don't watch the programming. A great church preacher talking to a congregation of TV watchers is a big damn waste of time. Remove TV programming first and then begin removing all of the sedatives and anxiety causing habits that poor people share in common. If the poorest and least healthy people all do something, then I try to avoid sharing their failing coping methods. Heavy TV watchers believing that they're spiritually connected because they attend church, is a joke. If this is you, then you're still a zombie.

It reminds me of a scene from "Indiana Jones and The Temple of Doom" when a sword fighter puts on a tremendous display of skill with his sword, and Indiana Jones simply pulls out his gun and shoots the swordsman dead! That's exactly what the TV set has done to the message of all organized religions. It's shot our consciences dead. Mr. Jobs obsessively dreamed of creating a hammer to take down old control systems; when paired up with today's internet, he did. Once again, the logo is an apple, and it's already been bitten. Jobs died young, but his hammer did strike the screen in time.

People who want truth above all else must unplug the cable cord. Television has been strangling all of our chances to take in so much as a spiritual breath. We don't try teaching calculus to our dogs, and shouldn't preach to TV zombies. End your own one-way relationship with a device that allows politicians to deliver their (hypnotic) speeches.

The visual power that a TV has when combined with the duration of viewing and sheer repetition of information shown is simply too powerful for the human brain to withstand. After side-stepping the billionaire prescribed brainwashing regimen of those other sub-par voters that we're disgusted with, our own brains will start to get stronger again. The thoughts and beliefs that run through our heads all day every day will suddenly start to become our own. The big joke about "paid" programming on TV is that all television is paid programming.

Movies are great metaphors and are a good substitute for somebody newly quitting their TV habit. People go through some serious withdrawals when they first quit. Quitting TV is no joke. Doing something for a lifetime and then suddenly stopping isn't comfortable. However, the brainpower that gets unleashed by doing so is well worth the first weeks of total weirdness.

Just like quitting anything else, you must have an attack plan. If you want to be successful, then prepare a replacement set of activities to fill the void that your TV created. You must ask yourself, has your life gotten better or worse from thousands upon thousands of hours spent motionless without being asleep in your bed? More terrifying, what if the billionaires have kept you asleep on your feet for all of these years? What if refusing to watch any television is like Neo being physically unplugged from the Matrix? If this is true, then unplugging people would be an honorable act.

You can only find out what happens by trying the experiment. Do you like the idea of a faster processor in your own head and a better body that results from hours of additional movement per day? Do you really want politicians and billionaires to continue controlling your thoughts, your actions and your beliefs because they've paid for the TV time?

If somebody is even suggesting that I can unplug myself from the Matrix, then I'm at least going to give it a try. If you could be awakened to a whole new reality, would you take the red pill or the blue one? The red pill awakens you to a new reality and the blue keeps life exactly the same. Which would you choose given your current set of circumstances?

Removing TV, fluoride, and frequent alcohol from my diet was enough to awaken to a whole new level of consciousness in a matter of months not years. The old feelings of hopelessness and self-pity will get replaced with peace, confidence, and a clear conscience. You'll begin to see things in a brighter and more optimistic way. Over time, others will begin to want what you have.

If you're going to try to half-ass these clear-cut behavioral modifications, then you'll simply remain asleep with the rest of the voters. Essentially, you'll be just another zombie littering the aisles of Walmarts across this fallen nation. On a cake box, if there are seven ingredients and if you want to get the cake, (just like the one on the side of the box) then you put in all seven ingredients. You're being informed exactly how to unplug yourself from the controllers of our society. There are proven recipes on the side of the box and within this book. If you follow the directions perfectly, then you get the desired cake (boosted consciousness and better health).

Refusal to follow simple directions results in failure to achieve the same results. There will be a void created by removing these habits from your daily routine that must be filled with new activities. If you want higher consciousness, then out with the old and in with the new. When I finally surrendered to God and humbly asked for help, within days something inside of me guided me to walk over to the wall and unplug my TV cable. Much like in this book, another person then posed the question to me, "Why is it that you're constantly altering the state of your mind with drugs or alcohol?" Like many other people, I had no clue. I'd never thought about it until that exact question was posed to me by a complete stranger. At that time my ego had been beaten down to a level of reasonableness.

Only after complete destruction of my personal life had it become apparent to me that taking new actions were necessary. I wanted to escape the hell that I was in at the time and was willing to try anything. I'm extremely thankful for walking into a room full of spiritual (not religious) people that greeted me with smiles and laughter on the first day that I met them. They seemed to have consciences and I wanted what they had. Most importantly I was willing to follow their directions. They didn't judge me for my mistakes because they had made similar ones in their pasts.

Don't most of us want something more, or something better out of life? Much like in high school, college, and at jobs, I asked questions. Lots and lots of questions. I can only describe what happened to me as a spiritual awakening. That's how it feels when you begin to get your consciousness turned back on again; it feels good. After a lifetime of having the goodness (connection to God) beaten out of us, wouldn't it be nice to feel some innocence again? I did.

People start to feel better just by having you in the room with them; people of faith that is. The other bazaar effect that happens as the goodness inside of all of us (our conscience) gets turned back on again is that people that are angry with God or totally worship money seem to flee the room with fear. It's as if sociopaths are naturally repelled once you've removed yourself from the zombie diet. We do live in a polarized world.

Abusive people and frauds don't know what it is, but they're naturally pushed away from high levels of consciousness. Those of us that unapologetically wield the truth, wield a sword that evil men will always fear. We must simply swing it. If there's one thing that frauds in our lives fear the most, it's the truth (so speak it already). Frauds should be uncomfortable, don't forget that.

Try speaking the truth more frequently. When we do so, frauds in our presence will have nowhere to feel safe. If we're God fearing people that have always longed for a world where the good guys are running the show, then perhaps we should stop kissing the asses of wealthier people (that clearly lack consciences). Failing to

166

call out frauds on their lies to their faces is simply perpetuating their comfort. Don't allow it. Be the sun around shady people.

It's time that we stop doing things that cause us anxiety (starting with our morning coffee). This is one thing that many of the stupidest and most fearful Americans share in common. Of all of the most ignorant people that you actually know, how many of them drink coffee daily? Find the most intelligent and physically fit people that you know and ask them what they do daily. There are plenty of non-coffee drinkers in America that happen to be very fit. Before you throw this notion out of the window, try it for three weeks and see if you don't feel less anxious. Alternatives do exist.

Why on earth would any self-respecting person continue on (in a crooked system) as a lowly voter? Walk into health food and vitamin stores and ask the fit people inside what they're doing differently. Chances are that they don't follow the same daily routine as the crippled and bloated grocery-store-limpers that we all see weekly. The walking dead do exist.

Chapter 16 – Secret Weapons Of Mass Sedation And The Hidden History Of NASA

The water being used to make your morning coffee and cook your food with is another thing that the ignorant masses share in common. Joseph Stalin and Adolf Hitler both introduced fluoride into the drinking water after their top scientists discovered its subduing effects on mass populations of people. Stalin found that the number of prison guards could be reduced by 75% after introducing fluoride into the inmates water supply. Cha-ching!

How many billionaires do you think drink unfiltered tap water in their mansions? All of our nervous systems operate using electrical impulses including our hearts and brains. We all have an electrical charge for every thought and heartbeat. Minerals and metals found in our tap water have a much larger effect on all of us than we've been led to believe. Just add tap water to a lead battery if you'd like to ruin it. Is this making sense?

Anyone that knows anything about cars knows that old car batteries sometimes need water to be added to them. The water added must be distilled, not tap water because the minerals found in tap water will wreck the battery. Any mechanic knows this. It also turns out that fluoride isn't good for the electrical conductivity in our brains. Drinking fluorinated water makes it a little harder for us to concentrate and remember things.

More disturbing is the fact that barrels of fluoride must be labeled as a hazardous waste. These barrels are then shipped as a waste product from factories and then dumped into our treated city water. It makes all of us that drink it daily, just a little dumber. This is also true with the fluoride in our toothpaste twice a day, every day. Congrats comrade.

In the light of certain facts being revealed to a zombie (not you of course) still heavily under the influence of weed, alcohol, TV, pills, and fluoride, to continue on changing nothing is only possible if we then exercise one of life's greatest sins, willful ignorance. It's unlikely that a proud idiot would be this far along in this book. It's my belief that as human beings, we came here to explore. We all fully have the right to purposely get as lost as we want to for as long as we want.

We all have the right to continue on as other people's servants that call ourselves victims. We can continue to wait for someone else who's less drunk, less drug-addicted and more self-respecting than us to come along and save us. I've explained the fluoride revelation to my own parents. The response from my 76 year-old father (health deteriorating, diabetic and currently captured by the immense gravity of the American armchair) was quite fitting. He walked over to the tap, poured himself a large glass of fluorinated water, and drank it.

I don't blame him, he's old, and has lived a long and fulfilling life. Both him and my mom are ready to go. My father has spent a lifetime fighting hard against evil and telling the truth at all costs. He's a good man that's given generously throughout his life. Most Americans are good people that have had their consciences hijacked with box-cutters and flown into buildings.

We all as a group have become just like my father (myself included) for a very long time. TV programming has trained us to throw the keys unlocking our own personal jail cells of ignorance and apathy right out of our cells. That programming is being broken.

As a child, my parents had both taught me to be uncompromising when it came to telling the truth. My father fought many battles against crooked business men always choosing integrity rather than compromising his honesty for financial gain. Over the course of decades as the city of Cleveland, Ohio steadily declined, telling the truth became a greater and greater liability. As corruption moves in, truth moves out. Don't give up. Keep speaking the truth and you'll be ejected out of corrupt places or will help to clean them up. It won't be easy, but it will be worth the struggle for future honest souls. God helps those that show some balls while shining brightly.

Many decent adults across America have retreated to the shelter of their family rooms. We've dove into pill bottles and weed

169

to avoid addressing the changing landscape of America. The increasing pile of lies referred to as the news has required increasing amounts of drunkenness for us to keep believing in. Many don't, and they shouldn't. An awakening public is beginning to catch staged lies at an ever quickening pace. An attack in Syria is found out to be old footage from a Kentucky gun show. Google it. The internet can run circles around the news just as Neo did around his opponents in the Matrix. Steve jobs killed TV.

Politicians on TV have no problem living their lifetime as a tiny ruling class over a country of poor hopeless drunks and drug addicts. That's pretty much what's happening right now. The recommendations that are extremely necessary for boosting your brain function are easy to implement.

The water you drink daily must be heavily filtered or distilled to remove all of the fluoride and glyphosate. Remember, distilled water in car batteries equals higher voltage and longer battery life. Running a human body on contaminated tap water is like running a car on dirty motor oil. Everything breaks faster. The water change is not an expensive one and is well worth it. Our ability to think more clearly and concentrate better occurs quickly.

There are holistic dentists out there that also disapprove of fluoride toothpaste. If you don't believe this, then Google it and do some research. Billions of people live fluoride-free and they aren't missing or losing their teeth any faster than the rest of us. Vitamin D from sunlight and diet has a lot to do with our dental health. No other mammal on earth requires fluoride for their teeth. Too much fluoride has also been linked to joint pain and inflammation.

Humanity went on for thousands of years without fluoride being added to our water. Suddenly, right after Hitler is defeated and thousands of Germany's top scientists were granted immunity and moved into the U.S. to work for our government; then, the U.S. begins the process of water fluorination. It's called Operation Paperclip. Look it up. The entire U.S. rocket program was created by ex-Nazi Germans.

The head of the U.S. Space Program after the end of World War II was named Wernher Von Braun. He and other former Nazis created what later became known as NASA (Nothing Actually Space Associated). Some of this information has actually been revealed by the History channel by a well done series called Ancient Aliens. Read the inscription on Wernher Von Braun's tombstone. It's another hint for the zombies only after his death.

Our governments and the kings have gone to great lengths to withhold information from the public. It's time that Americans realize that a whole lot of Nazis were welcomed into the U.S. following World War II. The control systems of Hitler's dreams (along with the men that were building them) didn't all die down in a bunker in Germany.

Chapter 17 – Politics, Religions, And Addicts

It's about time that we started uniting Americans in the United States. There's a lot more common ground that the masses do agree upon than our TVs and the people on them have led us to believe. Don't kill, don't steal, and don't answer honestly when a woman asks you about her jeans making her look fat. We get it.

How has it come to be that each presidential election divides the American people into a near perfect 50/50 split? In a true act of self-defeating insanity, the winning party then takes office after every single election and completely fails to deliver on any of their promises. We didn't bring home the troops in 2008 nor have things gotten any better for the (previously comfortable) middle-classers. The Affordable Care Act isn't affordable, and my grocery store workers are still missing teeth. None of the major campaign promises made by the candidates on either side ever deliver.

Pride prevents the completely dissatisfied voters from admitting that their winning candidate has completely abandoned all values and ethics that they believed they had. The result being that our personal pride has kept us trapped in these four year relationships with unfaithful partners. We keep on making excuses for them, even though everybody from the opposing side is pointing out the blatant lies. This applies to both parties. Acccpt this truth or remain a zombie with a crashed hard drive.

Stop believing that your politician is going to be different this time. It's like we're all betting on rattlesnakes not to eat the mice right in front of them. Please don't try telling me that things will be different after this next election. The lives of millions of people get harder while several hundred high-ranking politicians become wealthier. Nothing ever gets easier for us (the general public) while our rulers get wealthier. We're sliding into a tyranny. As tyranny rises, poverty increases. What's it going to take, 100 million U.S. citizens on food stamps for us to realize that criminals are running the scam?

This sounds like a winning strategy for a country of people that are now being heavily oppressed between (and during) elections. Proud citizens with their noses in the air (and their chins held high) are asking to wake up on the canvass. What do you think the German citizens were like after Hitler's fall? Stubborn pride and willful ignorance sets up apathetic citizens for a rude awakening.

The exact same phenomena occurred during the George W. Bush presidency that's happening right now under Obama. We the voters are to blame for this ongoing abusive relationship. Our own lack of self-respect is the only thing keeping us all from firing our corrupt leaders now. They're not leading us well. We do have the power to remove all of them from office at once. We also have the right to do so. They're employed by us, and we can remove them from power. This did happen recently in Iceland, but you'll never hear that concept on TV.

Have you ever seen somebody getting cheated on by their spouse that probably knew it deep down inside, but was too afraid to end the relationship? Do you respect people like that more or less for failing to confront (and lose) a disloyal partner? The American people have repeated the exact same prideful behaviors during the last 2 presidencies.

That's 16 long years of decline for baby-boomers' children that fell short of their parents' success levels. The rules all changed concerning job stability, decent wages, and housing prices. Nothing's worse than knowing that you've disappointed your parents in spite of doing your best. Once again, zombies are real and they'll bite anything with a conscience. We can build ourselves back up again by working hard and remaining honest.

Both Bush and Obama got re-elected after completely disappointing their own fan base during their first terms. Both Democrats and Republicans have been trained like dogs to never vote for the other party. Keep on accepting that only two terrible choices exist because this is the best treatment that we deserve. Shut up, and take your crappy circumstances for the next few years. Maybe your children will have the bravery to confront criminal dictators during their lifetime.

You might as well stay with girlfriend A that's cheating on you because girlfriend B would cheat on you even more often. To both politicians and strippers, money is God. Their spiritual connection that would consider the best interests of humanity isn't turned on. They shouldn't be our leaders. It's time that the public fires all of the corrupt officials and installs new rules that benefit hardworking people. We can do this, and we don't have to wait until another election to fire corrupt representatives. They do work for us and we've forgotten that.

If Americans weren't drinking and pill-popping ourselves into the walking dead, then we would've stopped buying the delusional version of reality a long time ago. Both the stripper and the politician aren't interested in us. They don't care about us, and when our money runs out, they'll leave us for dead. This is reality. This is the truth. These types of multiple-year agreements and the people that have been pursuing them need to be replaced. Retired Americans across the nation sit at home silently while their working-aged children slip further and further into drugs and alcohol to tolerate the brutal job market that normal people are barely surviving in.

Ron Paul won the Texas straw poll in 2011 and in 2012 for the Republican nomination. He was a shoe-in for the presidency if he'd won the nomination for his party, but he wasn't allowed to. Ron Paul didn't support the agenda of the billionaires that now own both parties. Therefore, a much weaker candidate was picked for the 2012 election cycle by the powers-that-were. The powers that truly control Congress and the White House don't give a crap who the American public agrees with the most. Obama doesn't call the shots. He's just the spokesman to sell the public the next round of well-crafted lies.

Did you really believe that Bin Laden was dumped at sea? Do you know that the entire Seal Team that "got" Bin Laden was killed in a helicopter crash because they were telling their families a different story? We're equally as gullible as the public from "The Running Man" when it comes to buying televised propaganda that makes our government look like our protectors. They don't protect, they collect.

From the point that Mitt Romney was falsely installed as the best chance for the Republicans to retake the White House, the smartest and most critically-thinking members of the American middle class had been taken out of the race. The independent voters were told loud and clear that our billionaire owners are nominating the candidates that they want to. Independent thinkers need not apply, and our election process is a fraudulent joke.

There's a youtube video featuring a former Russian KGB agent explaining how to transition a country into a dictatorship (without the citizens noticing). The video was filmed in the 1980's and clearly outlines how mass populations can be demoralized (have their morals removed) and molded over the course of a generation. It's called, "Four steps to subversion of a nation." It's a prophetic warning from somebody that actually escaped from an actual socialist nightmare. People within the government agencies steal everything while the majority of the public lives in total poverty. This isn't complicated stuff, and we're not supposed to fall for the same con now that it's been identified.

Zombie Americans will keep riding a sinking ship right down to the bottom of the ocean. We have a duty to our fellow man to get our own shit together. Too many Americans have been led astray by a grossly underestimated tool of influence called TV. Corrupt billionaires have gained full control of TV content and have peddled an entire buffet of consciousness killing substances to the public. In order to receive some divine intervention, we must first break the spell of TV. We don't have to achieve perfection in all areas, but we can improve.

I see lots of grown adults that are limping about their daily lives after years of hard work and regular attendance at some type of organized religion (for one hour per week). I'd argue that these people are running on spirituality 1.0 vs. TV 7.0 and are a completely indoctrinated group of marks. If God is all powerful and we greatly believe, then why can't God help us to control how often we eat, or how much we weigh?

It's not God that has failed to give us self-control; it's the TV that's taken it away from us. The vast majority of Americans would likely agree that they believe in God and would really like some help from said God with today's problems. Many Americans have lost so much in such a short time, that they'd like to see some revolutionary changes. We can do this peacefully, but don't have to continue being polite toward criminals.

Imagine that an armored guard comes into your place of business in their street clothes and demands something that your boss doesn't approve of. We then pepper-spray them in the face because they disagree with our owners, and then have them arrested for civil disobedience. That sounds fair enough, right?

Only a country of zombies would watch the 99% protesters get brutalized on TV and do nothing. How could we not demand that all of the armored soldiers and their bosses that gave the orders to pepper-spray not get prosecuted for terrorizing the American public? We all watched, and then quickly retreated into the safety of our houses like the obedient dogs that we've become. That is, until our houses got taken away by the same bankers that own the armed guards in the streets.

Should we just leave dictators in power forever and sit high or drunken on our couches watching sports and waiting for Jesus? Correct me if I'm wrong, but Jesus mostly gave people verbal advice. He wasn't an action hero that flew around the world like Superman; he gave logical spiritual advice, stayed poor, and (allegedly) performed miracles that no mortal voter will ever be able to reproduce. Does that sound about right?

If you're waiting for Jesus Christ or Superman to be actually standing right beside you before you're willing to do something courageous, then you have nothing brave about you. What if the Roman Emperor did successfully construct the Bible through control of the priests 300 years after Christ died? What if governing officials inserted miracles into the story of Christ because after doing so, no man, no matter how honest, brave, fast or strong would ever be able to walk on water? Essentially, they constructed a social control program that would stop all future generations from revolting against tyrannical leaders and the church. No living man could reproduce the miracles of Christ to rally living Christians against the forces of evil. Instead, we should have some wine and wait for a more powerful savior to come and save us.

King James could easily rule over Cleveland, Ohio, but in the system that we now live under, he too has somebody that signs his paychecks. When he says something out of line, a female sportscaster tells him to "Shut up and dribble." Yikes. Imagine Mr. James in Medieval times leading an army into battle against average-sized people. Coming face to face with an armored LeBron would be horrifying. Bankers that are normal-sized (like the rest of us) should fear doing harm to millions of increasingly poor sports fans (but they don't). Bankers are backed by the almighty dollar (which trumps Christ) so our modern day giants work for them.

Is it possible that the Bible was edited in a way that would make all future Christians wait (without taking action) for the return of their savior while getting their asses kicked by the current government? Would an Emperor tamper with history and have his own priests mass produce books that convinced the general public to perpetually wait for a savior (that never shows)? This would allow for thousands of years of corrupt kings to rule uncontested. Elites struggle for worldwide control while the public sits in stands (eating $5 hot dogs with $7 beers). We're not marks at all.

Meetings of billionaires (that do take place) determine which direction the politicians will move the people each year. They call this meeting of billionaires The Bilderberg Group. It does exist. Google it.

Here we stand 2000 years after Christ with around 7 billion people that appear to be terrified of death and are ritualistically attending 1700 year-old belief systems that were created by Constantine to control very stupid people. How exactly would Jesus try to reason with us if he was here in today's world? If we want God's help to get us out of this terrible economy and help free us from crooked politicians, then we may actually have to show God a little bit of effort.

A lot of humbling things have happened to millions of good people since the crash of 2008. Many of us had slaved away for years of our lives to finally obtain that crowning achievement that was part of owning the American dream, homeownership. All of that stuff isn't who we are or what we're made of.

Like the three generations before us, we expected our lives to continue along a prosperous path with normal ups and downs. However, millions of lost homes since 2008 have rocked the psyches of our entire country. I'd argue that the billionaire bankers that have eluded justice thus far have made a fatal mistake. They took away too much, too fast, from too many God-fearing people (without finishing the job). Rather than crushing our will to have freedom, they've boosted the natural spirit within us. They didn't expect this because they lack the same spirit. Positive change will come from this, because you can't turn free men into slaves.

Nearly all of us have the potential to do something good for this world. Let's take advantage of this opportunity and begin using our strengths to help others. Let's remove comfort from the lives of our pyramid-scheme politicians.

Do you see God on TV? I see a false representation of reality. I see the illusion for what it is. We can undo tons of intrusive control systems that have been constructed while we've been asleep. Freedom awaits the brave and servitude awaits the cowardly.

Chapter 18 – Practical Actions For Positive Change

When you bake a cake, do you pick and choose which ingredients to put in it? Not if you actually want the cake to turn out like the one on the box. You must remove all consciousness killing substances that have been scientifically proven to reduce brain function. It's time to get your brain operating at full power again.

Things to remove:

- No TV for one month. Once you've gone a continuous month without it, you won't want to go back.

- No more fluoride, this means no fluoride toothpaste, and no drinking or cooking with tap water. Buy distilled water or get a three stage water filter. Cheap filters don't remove fluoride. The health benefits will become obvious.

- For men that want to be masculine, eliminate soy protein from your diet. Soy acts as an estrogen mimicker. Read labels, you'll be surprised at how many foods have soy added to them.

- Cut alcohol to a minimum. If this sounds terrible and you're reasoning why you can't reduce your drinking, you may be an alcoholic and that's ok. Would it be so bad to lose dependence on alcohol? If you're addicted, then you may need some help to cut back. Set aside your pride and seek help if you need it.

- Stop popping mood altering pills unless you're a documented paranoid schizophrenic or a documented bi-polar person with a chemical imbalance. Only a tiny fraction of us truly need to be chemically sedated at all times. Working out releases anti-depressants the natural way.

- Try replacing coffee with something that health nuts use instead. There are plenty of caffeine alternatives available at supplement stores such as: 5 hour energy, Green Tea, or pre-workout supplements that will give you all of the kick of coffee with no unwanted anxiety and no yellowing of your teeth. Drink plenty of purified water during the day.

- A gallon of distilled water daily works miracles to detox an old body. Try it, and you'll be amazed after a month.

- Eliminate diet soda. The aspartame that's in it is terrible for your brain. Only with the right people in the FDA was aspartame made legal (during the Bush years). Severe negative health effects are documented in lab studies. Just because a product is legal doesn't mean that it's not also lethal.

Running plenty of distilled water through your system is absolutely essential for detoxing your body. Making these changes will help old dogs learn new tricks.

Things to add:

- Sleep, we all need it and our brains require a good night's sleep to flush out toxins that accumulate during the day. This is scientific fact. Sleep more and remember more.

- Exercise, you may have to actually work a little during the day in order to be tired out by bedtime. In moderation, exercise is very good for all of us. Workout a couple of days per week and walk daily.

- Positive music, find out what music the happiest people are listening to and avoid the same music that all of the poorest and dumbest people always have on. If you're listening to angry music, then you'll remain an angry person. Anger is often fear all dressed up.

- Walk.

- Read.

- Try new activities. Learning new things strengthens your brain. If you like singing, then sing! Some say that karaoke heals the soul.

- Be thankful. It's amazing, but just by thanking God for what you do have, you'll feel better. Try it.

- Get outside. We're not cave dwelling vampire bats! Enjoy a little sunshine; this world is beautiful. Sunlight releases large amounts of useable vitamin D. Vitamin D plays a huge role in our immune system and liver function.

- Forgive. When you forgive everyone who's ever done you wrong, you can finally forgive yourself for being human. Let the universe handle other people's bad behaviors but don't be a doormat. Stick up for yourself when needed, but avoid ongoing battles with assholes. Walk away.

- Don't stick around in bad situations to make sure that your oppressor gets punished. Walk away and let God handle it. Horrible people create horrible luck for themselves.

- Walk away from repeat abusers if they refuse to do what's right when confronted with the truth. Truth sets us free.

- Create a plan B and exercise your right not to be a victim for any longer. Ideas create reality.

- Laugh. On a planet full of hairless talking monkeys, it's much healthier to laugh at rather than getting angry at people. Anger kills good health.

If you're not already walking at least half a mile per day, then you'll need to add this very short walk into your daily routine. Why? Your body has to actually get moved a little in order to get fresh clean water distributed throughout your system. Cars that just sit in garages and never get driven fall apart. Both cars and people start to fall apart if they sit for too long. We all know this is true.

The radiator fluid in our cars becomes overly acidic and corrosive over time. The water in our bodies also needs to be swapped out on a regular basis to keep things running in tip top shape. Drinking something acidic in the morning isn't bad, but ten sodas per day will wreck most people's chances of having a good body. Good physiques paired with positive attitudes attract good company.

Health nuts drink tons of water and look healthy while bloated Walmart zombies drink sodas all day long. We're choosing what types of Americans we're copying on a daily basis. We all have created the body that we have. If it's in bad shape, then we can begin creating a better one today. Unless we're paralyzed from the neck down, we're determining the shape that we have. Removing TV removes hours per day of couch-ridden paralysis.

You don't have to continue mimicking insane behaviors that are repeated daily by unhappy people. New choices are now right in front of you. If you choose to take these new actions that result in a healthier you, then the world will begin rewarding you for doing so. Once you've successfully detoxed your body and your level of consciousness begins to rise, several amazing things will begin to happen:

- You'll begin to have more energy.
- You'll enjoy increased concentration and a boosted ability to solve problems.
- You'll feel more optimistic.
- You'll feel more loving and forgiving.
- You'll become more thankful.
- Abusive relationships will come to an end.

Your body will become more tuned to things that are good or bad for you, for example: Your skin may break out after eating toxic foods. Listen to your body and avoid foods and drinks that cause your body to negatively react. You'll gain a stronger intuition and naturally know when people are being both honest and deceptive toward you. Go with your gut.

This brings us to the metaphysical benefits that heightened consciousness provides to people. Buddhist monks are said to be walking around at a higher vibration than the average person does. What the heck does that actually mean? When someone's in love or you meet somebody that's very positive, you tend to feel their energy. Some people give off good vibes, and some don't.

Hateful people give off bad vibes and the people around them sense it. Monks have carefully trained their minds to focus on positive thoughts. Their bodies respond in a positive way due to an overall lack of stress. Gregg Braden is world renowned in the field of metaphysics, has written multiple books, and explains on YouTube how our DNA behaves differently according to our state of mind. Basically, the DNA in our bodies operates at its 100% God- given capacity if we're acting in a loving manner. Be kind and you'll be healthier.

The most energy is available to us if we're kind and forgiving on a daily basis. How many really selfish people do you know that have always had plenty of money but are always complaining about their bad health? Give generously without any ulterior motives and you'll begin to feel better about yourself.

Chapter 19 – Letting Go Of Stubborn Pride

It's never too late to become a better person. Humanity can't seem to ask God for help until we're heading over a cliff and that's ok, because it's how God made us. We don't deserve help if we completely sacrifice the whole group just to save our own asses. We must be willing to sacrifice our own safety and comfort in order to benefit the group (that's currently under great stress). In this matter, the present elites on planet earth are failing miserably.

The health of selfish people suffers and decent people disappear from their lives. Of course life seems very unfair, because other selfish people are the only ones that'll keep hanging around them. Money-worshipping people construct an entire existence that becomes void of decent people. The only willing takers are all spending time with them for the financial benefits and status.

Selfish people are clueless of the fact that reliable and honest people avoid them. This would be like a shark in the ocean that doesn't understand why the fish are always swimming in the opposite direction. We now hide at home all day watching TV to avoid scores of rude (unconscious) people limping through life trying only to survive. People that are following the herd mentality throw pills at things like heartburn.

Most Americans throw pills at everything. Can't sleep, a little pain, a little anxious, you name it and there are pills for it. Have you ever stopped and considered that pain in your chest is a biological response to let you know not to eat something again? It'll be easier to listen to your body after you've boosted your consciousness. We weren't designed like cows and pigs that eat all day long just waiting to be led to the slaughter.

In the "Resident Evil" movies there's an umbrella corporation (the government) that has unleashed a virus on the world that turns normal people into zombies. This virus is called the T-virus. It took me until the fourth Resident Evil movie to figure out the most obvious point of all of the movies: the T-virus (tyrant virus) that had been sold to all major world governments as a biological weapon is simply, TV.

Nobody's going to have a spiritual awakening with one hour of church a week vs. 21 hours of T-virus exposure. You'll remain a zombie. I also don't want to set-up people for life-long servitude in cult-like spiritual clubs like AA that will tell you that you're never cured. Many people have the power to address personal problems, put in some hard work and become a healthier person.

Whatever spiritual path you choose is up to you. When you're searching for enlightenment, your own truth will resonate. Remember not to go overboard. Mimicking the actions of Jesus Christ or Buddhist Monks that abandon all material possessions will only alienate you in today's money-driven world. Sitting around meditating all day and maintaining a small Christ-like stature will get a very negative reaction from the general public. The current cut-throat world that we now live in often attacks people that may appear to be weaker than themselves. Zombies that see you as physically and financially weak will do nothing but punish those undesirable behaviors. Be strong and healthy looking to avoid unwanted hostility. But, when surrounded by the dead, be dead.

Act like Christ, and you'll quickly get crucified by our society at large. My own personal experience has given me a loud and clear message that lifting weights and carrying around a little muscle (along with extra body fat) can be the entire difference between a completely hostile world, or a much easier ride with abundant opportunities. Appear to be strong and confident, and zombies will offer you more food, money, and romantic opportunities. Look weak and humble, and zombies will offer you a lifetime of suffering and poverty. Until the rules of this world have changed, you must do simple things that will help eliminate some of the hostile realities that do exist.

Millions of people will readily surrender freedom for safety (if they're kept fearful enough). This book has already broken through fear-induced walls in your mind. What do you think the repetitive images of 911 were all about? Was it really necessary to replay the images of the collapsing Twin Towers over and over again, hundreds of times across the board on TV eliciting a deep psychological (destroying our logic) and emotional response?

It would be as if your own child had been struck by a car and your captor made you watch the video of them dying over and over again. It wasn't at all necessary to watch that traumatizing image so many times. It was as if the intent of the people who control the media was to traumatize us all. Repetition has been used to install fear.

If someone trying to control you showed a video of a car smashing into your child that then got away; you'd likely feel nothing but anger toward that other driver (instead of thinking about if the information being shown to you was accurate or not). Any information given to you after the image of your child being struck would be clouded by anger. Would you travel to the ends of the earth to get justice? Thousands of extremely brave men and women did just that.

Do we all make sound and logical decisions when we're angry? How many times have you said or done something hurtful while you were angry? Did your brain and your critical thinking ability work at all once your emotions had been triggered? Didn't it take until you were calmed down to apologize and use logical thinking again?

Most of us don't think too well once our emotions have been triggered. Con-men know this and are masters of triggering your emotions. I'm telling you exactly how to get off of their shitty ride. We're talking about the primary delivery system of crooked politicians and world bankers. Kill the con-men dead by killing your TV.

A traumatizing image is like a computer program that knocks down your brain's firewall and corrupts the logic in your head with the weapon of emotion. Emotion overrides logic every time. Ever been in love? How many times have we seen politicians of the other party as our sworn enemies? How many times have their words made us angry? Any good salesman (con-man) knows that if they want to get the sale, then they've got to tap into the customer's emotions. I sold things for years and had a nice house in

186

a nice neighborhood by age 26.

Salesmen (politicians) are experts at getting an emotional response that takes down the customers' (voters') natural defenses. Has it ever occurred to you that the two opposing sides on TV may actually be working together as a team of con-men? You know, the good cop bad cop routine? Afterwards, they all laugh because the general public forms a majority opinion to approve the pre-planned desired direction that billionaire elites have already chosen for us to choose. Does that make sense?

The politicians from both parties have only one real job; to sell the public on the idea that we're choosing the course of action. For our politicians, it's a lot like playing a retarded kid at basketball and making the kid believe that he really won the game. The general public really is this stupid. Future generations will know how accurate this paragraph is regarding the current political system in America. The illusion must be revealed.

Would a politician show a disturbing image (like the twin towers collapsing on 911) to his people in order to obtain blind obedience? After the image was shown hundreds of times, we did just about anything to avoid additional attacks. None of us reading this would do such a thing, but that doesn't mean that Dick Cheney wouldn't. Pretending that there are no sharks in the ocean doesn't stop seals from getting eaten.

Would a person with any conscience at all even show such a disturbing image over and over again, unless they had a motive? The emotional trauma caused by the images of the collapsing towers on 911 was instrumental to close the sale on the Afghanistan and Iraq wars. We were closed. Have I ever been closed by an unethical salesman during my adult years? Yes. When will we admit that we've been conned, so we can quit doing business with con-artists?

Without the attack, the people never would have backed the aggressive Middle-Eastern invasion. If only "The Project For A New American Century" didn't exist prior to the 911 attacks, but it did. Would the greediest men on earth hide an entire scam behind a traumatizing image that no parent would even dare to dig up even five or ten years later? Admitting that we've been had and then changing course is what evolving people do. The general public is directly responsible for our own levels of freedom or servitude. Bravery is contagious, so be brave. Speaking freely is the easiest way to do so.

Chapter 20- Backward Programming

TV spins a deceptive web of beliefs that has placed money above all else. The Wizard of OZ was shown on a big projection screen making him appear to be more powerful than he really was. In reality, the wizard was just a rich old man that had put on a big show to intimidate (to make timid) others. World bankers are just that, greedy old men that the common man could beat to death in a one on one confrontation. An army of security guards is what protects the little men behind the big screens, not God. God has nothing to do with any of this. These particular men don't believe in God and don't believe that the rules of cause and effect apply to them. Turn off the big screen and suddenly you'll start to get back your freewill and some courage.

We must also break the spell of addictive insanity caused by mind-numbing substances. If it's a pill or drink that makes us feel ok amidst our horrible life situation, then it's not going to help us to escape from our current mess. The all-powerful wizard wants us to keep his big screen turned on at all times, pop miracle pills and drink snake oil that does nothing but slow us down every day. If you're not already one of the fastest and strongest members of our society, then perhaps daily sedatives are a bad idea.

You now know how to take the governor off of your own brain. Eventually this knowledge will spread to the armed guards that protect our kings (world bankers). Eventually the guards will stand down so that we may face our oppressors one on one, and face to face. Worldwide poverty isn't going to increase so that a tiny ruling class can feel like Gods. They aren't. Many of the world's wealthiest people have been treating the general public like animals.

The world elites are simply greedy people that have overstepped the boundaries of reasonable behavior toward the rest of humanity. It's time that this ridiculous behavior comes to an end. We can change this now, and you can fight on behalf of humanity. We're all contributing to make this world what it is. Let's make it a better place during our lifetime.

Our children deserve a less corrupted system to live in. The current system will only continue on for as long as the public fails to challenge it. We all have the power to change this. It's time to stop waking up in bed with the same set of problems as the day before. The question is, do we all just concede and admit total defeat like 50 million other Americans on food assistance or not?

Rich kids with multi-millionaire parents are simply too smart for the rest of us inferior Americans to fight against. They've assigned a lifetime's worth of heavy lifting onto the backs of the American public. The majority of working-aged people are now living in sub-par circumstances. One third of the population has been pacified via government checks based upon the labor of the other two thirds.

Do you really think that the government would allow cigarettes if they didn't produce the most profitable and obedient workforce? Coffee and cigarettes are like liquid and vapor uneasiness for a beat-down workforce of self-hating slaves. The rebellious act of smoking is exactly what the billionaire slave owners want. Note that right in the beginning of "1984", Winston smokes his Victory Cigarettes and then rewards his unbearable existence with some Victory Gin.

The world elites would prefer for all of the poor people to be completely addicted to anxiety causing substances. Then, these same people sedate themselves with nightly brain damage making them even easier to dominate the following day. These are weapons that weaken our will to escape bad situations. Keep following the homeless person's diet: Cigarettes, Coffee, and Alcohol.

If you want to terrify the elite, then address your own emotional damage and drop your chemical crutches. If Americans did this by the millions, the billionaires would be pissing their pants. In fact, they're already fleeing the United States and building rural compounds in places like New Zealand. Without drug and alcohol dependency, we get a hell of a lot faster and smarter. Disgruntled Americans that are still wrestling with old baggage have even been tricked into labeling themselves.

Upper-class Americans remain tattoo-free, and the increasingly beat-down working class has illustrated their toughness via ink. Just because I'm not all marked up with warning labels to illustrate my rebellious nature and a wild past doesn't mean that I haven't lived it. Our churches betrayed us all by teaching us about a perfect human that never made mistakes. If Jesus Christ were here on earth right now, then he'd sure do us all a huge favor by letting us know that he made all of the same mistakes as the rest of us while living the human experience.

It's my own impression that governments put together the impossible guilt factory of unobtainable religious standards on purpose. This is all so that the ownership-class can step on poor people's toes all day long without getting punched in the stomach. My goal isn't for angry mobs of poor people to attack billionaires, they've prepared for that. It's for poor people to empower themselves so quickly on such a massive scale that all true criminal billionaires see no way out but suicide. Men like Hitler, Stalin, and the bankers that funded them would best serve this world by leaving.

We've all been set up for guilt by an impossible to obtain standard of purity; a standard more likely put into place by the Roman Empire, not by Jesus. Jesus didn't sell guilt; he sold forgiveness. The Roman Empire that evolved into the current Catholic Church and the Jesuits have had a much larger role in the world banking system than the zombie public understands.

Royalty hijacked the name of Jesus for their own money and control. It's time for a worldwide comeuppance for unholy people that have badly taken advantage of our dimwitted group. As a small percentage of our group awakens, the elites same old scams become more and more obvious. The awakened people point out shams to the rest of the public, and even more people begin to wake up.

For those of us that don't enjoy daily beatings or screwing over others for money all day long, there's now a key to remove our own mental shackles. If you'd like to take the governor off of your own brain, you now can. It's not the tattooed, beer-drinking rednecks in America that are the most damaged people. They're not. In fact, they're actually the strongest and most threatening group to the elites in America. The middle management suit-wearing corporate Americans that live in the suburbs are by far the most castrated non-threat to the growing tyranny in America. Rednecks fear nothing, and have more common sense than upper class Americans could ever comprehend.

Our society seems heavily-impaired regarding our learning curve when it comes to trusting in well-spoken men with conservative haircuts wearing expensive suits. What do all of the guys from "The Wolf of Wall Street" wear? Who else wears expensive suits and has conservative haircuts? Aren't most of the momentous lies and screw-overs committed against us in life perpetrated by men lacking tattoos and wearing suits? The whole clean-cut and well-spoken image means nothing. It is and always has been an illusion of purity.

I was always a clean-cut and well-spoken guy, but when it comes down to purity, it turns out that I'm perfectly flawed just like the rest of you. I'd more likely get described by most people that knew me prior to late 2011 as "A piece of work." 8 years later, I still am. I'm likely near the range of a high-functioning autistic person (kind of like Sheldon from "The Big Bang Theory" during my youth). I'm a bit eccentric, and there's no getting rid of it.

Over the years, negative aspects of my own personality (that needed to go) were let go of, and aspects of those that I've loved the most have grown within me. When you love someone so much that you can't live without them, the best parts of those people grow within you after losing them. Miraculous growth can follow great losses.

We've all been born here with many strengths and weaknesses. The biggest gift that we can give to one another is admitting our faults and helping other people to forgive themselves for being human. Our imperfections are woven together with our individuality and strengths. Being told that we're all equal is simply not true.

It takes a variety of different personalities to make the world run. Civilized coultures with kind people do allow individuality.

192

Beware when equality is offered by socialist-leaning leaders. Before you know it, they'll try to paint all of the birds in the forest the same color. Red.

Natural variation in human beings is as varied and as beautiful as in all other animals in nature. Just picture the massive variation in our dogs. They're all different shapes, sizes, and colors; yet they're all still called dogs. Different people see beauty in different ways. Beware if someone tries to tell you that we should all eat the exact same (school) lunches. Before you know it, your brainwashed neighbors will be beating you into conformity.

Societal rulers have constructed certain tools to make shady individuals appear more legitimate while simultaneously beating-down the confidence of good souls. There are plenty of good souls here on earth, on the ground, and ready to defend the innocent. Don't be fooled by men in suits. A suit is simply a ceremonial outfit that we've been trained and conditioned to trust. Recently, Brian Williams was exposed to be just another face you should trust (but shouldn't). He lied about being shot down in a helicopter in Iraq. He later apologized after being caught.

If anything, the American public should abandon the tradition of suits because they make sociopaths appear to be self-respecting people. The body beneath the suit reveals a lot more about a person's level of self-respect and self-control than the clothing that they're wearing. Put all of our governing officials in white tee-shirts and shorts and then see if the public believes their speeches.

The expensive suits and makeup for TV transforms Walmart people into royalty. It is all an illusion. Our Politicians are nothing more than smart people that are completely full of crap. Our political leaders seem to have lost their ability to tell the truth. They don't serve the God that I believe in, and I wasn't put on earth to serve them. There are actually more good people out there than bad. Let's serve the good ones.

Most Americans agree that screw-up rich kids shouldn't be the leaders of our country. However, when money buys votes, (and we all know it does) and parents want to see their otherwise screw-up kids succeed; then the possibility of screw-up rich kids becoming our only choice in a declining economy (much like Cleveland) increases with each generation. We know this has happened nationwide.

Had President Bush's family not been extremely wealthy, then he never would have stood a chance on the political playing field (due to his lack of speaking skills). His complete absence of job qualifications should have allowed for other more intelligent and well-spoken candidates to out-compete him. However, his father, former President, and former Director of the CIA paved the path for a non-qualified candidate. We all suffered the consequences (except for the 1%).

For decades the American public has been posed with two terrible choices for President, a bought off Congress, and sell-out Supreme Court justices that make decisions such as: A corporation is equal to a person. The American public has remained too high to get off of their couches during all of this. We're entirely to blame for remaining completely apathetic while the entire political system's been anally raping us.

Either Republican or Democrat, it doesn't matter. Both sides have been bought-off by one group of elites, not two. That's the huge joke that the zombie public doesn't seem to get. The whole control-system sham is finally nearing its end. It's our duty to make sure that more honest people take over the wheel. Believing in the two party systems continued effectiveness is like believing in the pull-out method of birth control. Only monkeys that can talk would believe in such a notion.

There's a Tri-Lateral Commission and an organization of billionaires that collaborate with each other determining world policy each year that's called the Bilderberg Group. They believe that they have the right to determine the policy that governs all citizens on earth (without consulting us). These groups ensure that they control either presidential nominee, because both nominees in every single presidential election are connected to both groups.

Which mafia guy are you going to vote for this year, the Republican or the Democrat? The two "opposing" candidates from

194

the same club have a huge laugh in private after putting on theatrical performances on television. They all work for the same gang and likely make fun of the moronic public that can't figure out the con. We're all seriously as dumb as a planet of talking primates, but that too is beginning to change.

For years of my life I watched other salesmen take customers on an emotional ride, dismantle their defenses, and then sell them something they didn't need or want. A skilled salesman using a barrage of logic on a customer is like a computer hacker breaking into your home PC and installing a virus program that takes control of your computer (all without your knowledge or consent). That's exactly what politicians are, front-men (and women) for the billionaire owners of this planet.

The politicians work for and fear the billionaire committee, not us. The politicians that have been running the country are simply front desk workers that are doggishly doing as they're told by the ownership committee of billionaires. They do this for fear of economic loss or personal injury; that, and massive blackmail. This all takes place at the expense of billions of people worldwide. This is changing.

As citizens, the only way to get any real solutions to our problems is to get past the cashier at the front desk. We need to have a chat with the greedy owner that hides in the back room behind closed doors that is busy counting his giant pile of money. Troops worldwide will have to stand-down to allow citizens to face their oppressors. As the citizenry closes in on criminals in power, more terrorist attacks will occur, followed by troops on the streets. Both the troops and the citizens must be conscious to avoid living in tyranny. Awareness is our key to freedom.

The owners do exist, and I have zero respect for them because they treat most of the public like cattle. Armed guards aside, the billionaire elites of planet earth are just a person having a human experience. They're not gods. There's a huge difference between true bravery and paid-off security. Many of these heavily-armed security guards have extended families and old friends that are beginning to suffer badly due to their bosses' actions.

If it becomes obvious that a leader has become drunken with power, (while the whole country suffers) then the public must demand their resignation. Election isn't a one-way street. Allowing a beautiful country to be openly dismantled for years at a time is an absurd notion. The public has the power to fire elected officials before their terms have ended. Otherwise, we're living in a dictatorship.

Chapter 21 – Excusers And Producers

If spiritual beings did come down to earth and quietly walked through a Walmart, (unseen and unnoticed) what would they say about the shoppers in front of them? Picture the typical Walmart shoppers and think of the way that they carry themselves. If spiritual beings did show up here on earth and offered us nothing but spoken advice on how to help ourselves, would we follow it?

Please consider that the majority of human beings have spent this lifetime praying to God to help us in this experience. What if bad guys on earth are simply exercising their rights of freewill? Why would advanced spiritual beings reward the cowardly behaviors of billions of people? Those of us that act like cowards in our daily lives get all of the fruits that cowards (cow-herds) deserve. Do you wish to be herded? Me neither.

Good parents that are trying to raise respectable children don't reward cowardly actions. When somebody acts like a bully toward the rest of the group, then we should hold them accountable. We shouldn't let a few bad eggs continue to bully the rest of us. Attempt to fight a seemingly undefeatable enemy (on behalf of humanity) and we might start to comprehend moments of divine intervention. They do exist.

Do you want to be a crippled victim of life when the angels ask how you did? Try some positive inputs and you might start to become more hopeful. Positive music not found on the radio can have a vastly uplifting effect on your mood. Music is powerful.

Believing in some sort of good intelligence beyond that of man isn't a bad thing. The alternative is to believe that money is God, and that kissing the asses of wealthy men in order to survive in a totally corrupted system is the pinnacle of all creation. I know that there's more than this, and I'm going to be part of the resistance (Muse album title).

Disasters in our lives aren't a good thing; they're a great thing because they cause intense pain. Pain then causes us to seek change. We're all capable of changing for the better. When was the last time that the public was all sold hope and change on our television? Those of us that grew up in comfortable middle class homes and were beaten into lower class lives remember.

The hope and change promised to us never really manifested itself. Working people are now worse off while welfare cheats keep raking in unwarranted benefit checks. When socialist policies get cranked-up, workers' motivation get's turned down. I've personally worked with such people. We're at a juncture in history where cheaters are winning and winners are losing. It's up to us to call out scumbags every step of the way. We must save ourselves.

America is sick and we need to seek help. Not from evil men, but from God. Not at a church, but from within you. You don't need some guy in a fancy outfit to talk to God for you. Help those who need help directly and cut scam artists out of your life. Be kind to those that are actually working hard and share your strengths with them.

We've all been throwing food, weed, pills, and alcohol at the symptoms, but the relief is only temporary. Fantasizing about brief escapes (while spending the majority of your time serving politicians that you don't even respect) is a pathetic way to exist. We're part of a herd of people that's over 300 million strong. Unchain yourself by turning off the delivery system of all billionaires' programming (TV).

Unscrew your cable box and begin tackling the substances that do nothing but knock you out. We can easily trample a few wolves that are systematically sedating us, and then feeding on us while we sleep. They want to thin the herd, and soon. Let's expose fraudulent leaders and watch them panic (already happening).

The T-Virus is stronger than most of us gave it credit for. At this point, most of the U.S. population's logic has been crippled by it. This T-Virus (TV) causes people to become fat, dumb, submissive, delusional, poor, and gives the victim an overall feeling of hopelessness.

What we don't see is that many of us are slowly becoming them. After all, we've all been exposed to the same virus. We can separate from the herd by abandoning the same daily habits as the rest of them. Obvious choices have been placed in front of us. We must cure ourselves first in order to become something that the T-virus zombies will want.

A healthy person that's full of life is hard for the T-Virus zombies to ignore. When we follow these stupidly simple directions, we will transform ourselves back into the spiritual creatures that many children still are. Don't many little kids possess a sense of innocence and a sense of goodness that most adults wish they still had? We can all get that feeling back by doing the right thing and helping our group.

As we raise our level of consciousness, we'll naturally want to help others that need it. Americans need our help right now because millions of them are suffering badly. We know this is true and we're not powerless in this struggle. Become someone that they want to be, and then show them what you're doing differently. We need to share our strengths with others, and can only do so if they want what we have.

Without first surrendering to God and asking for help, the battle is unwinnable. It may sound ridiculous, but it sure as hell has helped me. May you soon see the good side of humanity and soon see the good <u>all</u> of those other dirty voters. It's time that we start working together to fix problems that are threatening our entire group.

The end.

<u>Special Thanks</u>

Only through the work of pioneers in the field of consciousness have I been able to gain a more thankful perspective for my own life. The work of George Carlin, Alex Jones, Bill Hicks, and David Icke will forever be appreciated by me. These people openly challenged the status quo. They've absorbed a lifetime of hardships and ridicule because their thoughts were ahead of their time. Also, John B. Wells and the Caravan To Midnight radio show was the first widespread media outlet to stick their necks on the line by discussing an earlier version of this book.

I thank all men and women that have refused to conform in order to protect the freedoms of their neighbors. I'd also like to thank my parents for being extremely honest, forgiving, and generous to strangers while I was growing up. My parents repeatedly demonstrated unconditional love toward not only their family, but to humanity in general. My father has always been uncompromisingly honest and incredibly generous to both family and strangers.

Michelle and her insane redneck family will forever be loved by me. The best parts of them helped fuel the seemingly impossible journey that's created this book. I'll miss them always and look forward to seeing them on the other side. It was because of my love for them that this book was created. As a result, real people (after reading this book) have escaped from some terrible situations. Decent people deserve safety and comfort. Wicked people should live in fear, not the good ones.

There's hope for all of us. Men and women with good consciences can lead our group in a better direction. We're all collectively creating the world that we live in. Let's create something good that God would be proud of. Let's all start creating some better luck for ourselves by working hard and doing what's right more often.

200

Please Share This With Someone That'll Appreciate It.
Thank You,
Max

Made in the USA
Middletown, DE
12 December 2020